The Skin Above My Knee

The
Skin

Above My
Knee

A Memoir

Marcia Butler

Little, Brown and Company

New York Boston London

Little, Brown and Company
Hachette Book Group
1290 Avenue of the Americas, New York, NY 10104
littlebrown.com

First Edition: February 2017

Little, Brown and Company is a division of Hachette Book Group, Inc. The Little, Brown name and logo are trademarks of Hachette Book Group, Inc.

The publisher is not responsible for websites (or their content) that are not owned by the publisher.

The Hachette Speakers Bureau provides a wide range of authors for speaking events. To find out more, go to hachettespeakersbureau.com or call (866) 376-6591.

Lyrics to "Optimistic Voices" on page 63 copyright E. Y. Harburg.

Excerpt from "I Am Lost" on page 183 copyright Bruce Gilmour.

ISBN 978-0-316-39228-0
LCCN 2015960626

10 9 8 7 6 5 4 3 2 1

LSC-C

Printed in the United States of America

For Terril Gagnier
The mother I never had
The sister I dreamed of

Author's Note

The events in this book took place. As my memory is sometimes fallible, dialogue is approximate. Some names have been changed, and certain events have been reordered or compressed in order to serve the story. I've made best efforts to ensure accuracy of detail and emotion in the way I layered the two into this recounting of my life.

The Skin Above My Knee

Minnows

AUDIENCES MARVELED AT this young violinist—how he performed with effortless abandon, uninhibited by the technical challenges in the violin concerto repertoire. Tonight, our audience was newly enthralled, on the edge of their seats inside Carnegie Hall, as the Mendelssohn Violin Concerto moved at breakneck pace. In the principal oboe chair, alongside the fifty-plus other musicians in the orchestra, I leaned forward, listening intently, not wanting to miss a second of the violinist's nuanced interpretation. My eyes wandered over the conductor's head to the upper balcony of Carnegie Hall—137 steps above the lobby. The very first time I performed on this stage, so many years before, I'd also gazed up to the farthest patron. Young and new to the freelance scene in New York City, and fresh out of music conservatory, I remember pinching myself for my good fortune: I had made it to that venerable and most august of concert halls.

Years later, I felt I knew the Mendelssohn Violin Concerto almost as well as the soloist; I'd performed it within the orchestra dozens of times over many years. Considered to be perfectly constructed, this iconic work of the violin repertoire emerged from Mendelssohn's genius at age thirty-five. Unencumbered by compositional traditions of his time, he experimented with a concerto form in flux, ultimately becoming a critical composer in bridging the late-classical, muscular writing of Ludwig van Beethoven and what would become the lush and broadening romantic realm of Johannes Brahms. The violin concerto reveals what a precocious innovator Mendelssohn was, retaining the usual fast-slow-fast movements of classical concertos but breaking with form by having the soloist enter immediately at the beginning of the first movement rather than using a lengthy exposition by the orchestra to introduce the thematic material. All three movements are performed attacca, or without a break. Neither the violin soloist nor the orchestra has the opportunity to regroup after each movement, whether to retune or just relax. We begin, and then it is "go" until all noses cross the finish line. No matter how many times I'd performed that concerto, I felt compelled to jump out of my seat at the end along with the audience.

Along I played, in love with the soloist's interpretation of this warhorse favorite, feeling as if I were part of an intricate Flemish tapestry made of silky sounds and woolen harmonies. We musicians in the orchestra carefully balanced our accompaniment, and I emerged occasionally with my own solo here and there. The flow was instinctive, as if we could play it in our sleep. But not quite. Music of the late-classical period can be repetitive and easy to mix up because melodies are repeated many times and whole sections may be revisited, albeit in a different key. It isn't a matter of not knowing the piece well enough but of losing one's presence in time, or perhaps the mind's uncanny ability to function on different levels of consciousness simultaneously.

And when a long work is performed, the mind wanders to surprising and perhaps unimaginable places—almost like dreaming onstage.

Perhaps this particular conductor was thinking about the reception afterward and the donors he needed to chat up. He certainly wasn't thinking of the musicians before him, his arms offering us no assistance, his eyes shut as if enthralled. No matter. A conductor's public persona often trumps his conducting skills. Charming potential donors brings in necessary revenue, after all. And while he was no genius on the podium, we knew that this conductor could effectively execute the public "fearless leader" aspect of his job and guide us with minimal help.

Other minds also wandered. Just before stepping onto the stage, a section violinist had a screaming fight with her husband by cell phone. We had all heard it, trying not to listen too carefully. She surely had other things on her mind as she crimped her violin under her chin, preparing to play her next entrance. My eyes drifted toward a friend in the viola section. Our eyes locked. She signaled a very subtle "Oh, brother" look, lifting her brows slightly. I knew just what she meant: she detested this conductor. Glancing back over to the violinist who'd fought with her husband, I noticed her hooded and dull stare while she played a particularly difficult passage in a tutti section. Yet the music continued, beautifully.

I indulged in my own momentary lapse, wondering how my new puppy was doing and worried because I'd left her at home alone for far too many hours. Now the third movement was beginning, so I refocused and started diligently counting my rests, preparing for my next entrance.

Many complex lives wove snugly together on the stage,

and in spite of this communal daydreaming, the bitching and moaning by means of conspiratorial glances bandied back and forth, and the nonverbal high jinks, a wonderfully transcendent performance was emerging. Scattered minds and thoughts notwithstanding, we remained intensely occupied with the task at hand: the performance by a superb violinist and a sensitive and attuned orchestra of one of the greatest violin concertos ever written.

An orchestra functions not only on these levels but also as a tight, organic, undulating ball of kinetic energy, similar to an enormous shoal of minnows—thousands of which can span half a mile. Consider the whimsy of one minnow. Suddenly, that first minnow decides to make a 180-degree turn, and every single one of the others makes the same exact turn at precisely the same second. Spanning half a mile, where minnow number 1 can't even see minnow number 50,000, they pivot on an invisible fulcrum. This intuition is undoubtedly primal and surely important for their survival: it is also wondrous to watch. That evening, our soloist made his own whimsical version of a 180-degree turn, and we became his personal school of minnows. The first little fish veered, and an orchestra awakened.

We felt the subtle rupture in the music, not sure of what had happened or even if it was significant. But as it turns out, it was big: the violin soloist skipped eight bars, heaven only knows why. Daydreaming or just losing his place, he jumped and kept on playing as if nothing had happened. But what occurred next was unfathomable, really, except if you consider the humble minnow.

When the violinist made his error, the principal trumpet player instantaneously took on the role of minnow number 2. He had been counting many rests, waiting for an important entrance, but when the soloist leaped, he jumped, too, and put the trumpet to his lips to play his heralding entrance. He did this without thinking, it seemed, and in a split second. Upon hearing the trumpet entrance, half the orchestra jumped eight bars and followed him. By beat 4, all fifty-plus musicians were perfectly aligned. That was all it took: four very fast beats.

A small smile appeared on the face of the violin soloist as he realized what he'd done—and how the orchestra had saved his performance. Mendelssohn may have known from his grave that eight bars had been deleted from his magnificent violin concerto. But the audience was none the wiser, because those four seconds were a mere blip on the radar. Our conductor, whose eyelids were still fluttering and shut, listening to his internal and solitary rapture, was the last to catch up.

Compositions are painstakingly rehearsed in order to establish the basic interpretive arc for how the work will be heard by an audience. But in performance, many previously agreed-upon subtle details and gestures worked through during rehearsal may be spontaneously tossed out. Skipping eight bars of music aside, musicians love it when something unexpected happens. These moments are experienced as group impulses, emanating from the collective beating heart of the ensemble. Calling this nonverbal communication is too simplistic. It is not just an intuitive understanding among highly skilled artists but rather a developed, honed expertise realized after thousands of hours of practice and a lifelong dedication on the part of each musician to the mastery of his or her instrument. Musicians are gifted, no doubt, but they are also muscled Clydesdales. Perhaps it was our dogged preparation that helped dig the violinist out of his potentially embarrassing mess. A piece of music, played perhaps thousands of times before, can be interpreted spontaneously or manipulated quickly because of an error, a fact profound in concept and occurrence. And thrilling. We call this making music.

When we finished the Mendelssohn Violin Concerto, the ecstatic audience clapped with extended and then renewed force. The soloist came back for several bows and played an encore of unaccompanied Bach. We left the stage and filed upstairs to the dressing rooms, another concert at Carnegie Hall under our belts.

"Nice job, Bill," we simply said later to the trumpet player as he was packing up, getting ready for his commute home to Leonia, New Jersey. The section violinist had a make-up cry with her husband on the cell phone. I packed up my oboe quickly, rushing so that I could get home to let my pup out the door. The violin soloist didn't show up to thank the orchestra—or the trumpet player, for that matter. Our conductor was nowhere to be found.

As I walked out the stage door of Carnegie Hall with my friend the violist, she took up her rant about the incompetence of conductors in general. Nodding in agreement, I let her vocal treatise float into the background. I was already musing about the performance that evening, dreaming again about the first time I performed at Carnegie Hall and how in awe I was of the sheer beauty of the space and the impeccable, world-class acoustics. Even now, after my many years of performing concerts all over the world, Carnegie Hall still softly rocks me—suddenly I felt very young.

I noticed the quickening of a deep vessel expanding within my heart; always beating, always pulsing. Walking down the subway steps, I remembered the very day when my guileless four-year-old ears first experienced the life-altering impact of music. I halted midstep and stood, motionless, needing to grab that fleeting, now ancient, sensation; to hold it close again for just a moment. My heart slowed, aching for the next beat.

Hoover

WATCHING THE HOOVER sway back and forth across the living-room carpet, I lay flat on my back, my legs bent like a pitched roof. Loose, fuzzy tufts of the velvet-cut pile surrounded my head and tickled my nose, waiting to be sucked into the vacuum cleaner. A menacing rubber rope connected to the machine swung above me, snapping with a blurred smear. As I held my little four-year-old body very still, this lumbering machine moved toward then away from me, sounding like the bellows of a monstrous accordion. My mother deftly negotiated the space—rocking the vacuum and flipping the electrical cord over the sofa, over the club chair, over the lamps. Over me. The Hoover's wheezing rumble receded far into the background, the cord now a tolerable blur. But other sound clusters crowded, as *music* pressed closer—around me, over me, into me.

Our home on Sunday mornings in Pittsfield, Massachusetts, resounded with the conclusion of Richard Wagner's opera *Tristan und Isolde,* as Norwegian opera singer Kirsten Flagstad sang Isolde's final aria, the "Liebestod." It was 1959. "Liebestod" translates as "love-death," a complex concept sweeping far beyond my young capabilities, yet I implicitly understood this sung story to be simultaneously deeply sad and marvelously transcendent. Isolde stands over her dead lover, Tristan, and has taken poison that will hasten her own death in order to join him in the afterlife.

Dramatic sopranos gifted enough to sing the Wagnerian opera repertoire are rare indeed. The unparalleled Kirsten Flagstad, whose magnificent career waxed in the 1930s and waned in the early 1950s, was perhaps the rarest. All her vibrant vocal resonance was held in the facial mask, around the nose and eyes. Her voice was not at all nasal; she possessed a gloriously hollow quality. A once-in-a-century voice—never shrill, never mannered, and never what we have come to identify as "operatic."

A new and pleasurable sensation sank deep into my tummy, like a very heavy anchor with no water to resist its plunge. This squishy giddiness was as alive and direct a sensation as anything yet available in my young life. Kirsten shook me awake. With the distance of time, I suppose it was love. Kirsten *must* have loved me.

I was hooked. When the vacuum started and my mother dropped the needle onto the vinyl LP grooves, I'd race to the living room, dive-bomb onto the carpet, and settle into ten minutes of sentient comfort. It almost hurt, but it could not be ignored. Wagner's signature musical landscape was a backdrop onto which an aching melodic line could float—and then soar—telling Isolde's story through Kirsten's voice.

Kirsten sang:

Do you see it, friends?
Don't you see it?

As I listened to Kirsten and wondered what Isolde was singing about, I also ached for my mother, whose right hand remained at the top of her Hoover, the left tethered to the long electrical cord. By keeping us clothed, sheltered, and fed, she met our physical needs, but no additional juice came our way. We knew this, as children do, but just to press the seal onto the wax, we were told, often.

"Honestly, I don't know what is the matter with you girls. I don't play favorites. I treat you the same. You each get what the other gets. What more could you possibly want? *Please.*"

With this branded into my phyllo-thin skin, my mother was off to her bedroom with one of her frequent and debilitating migraines. With the door locked, curtains drawn, the house silenced, she mothered from a deafening distance. Our carefully deadened home, with a churchlike quiet, gave her comfort and provided the space she needed.

During the week I would discover many of the thin cracks and shallow crevices of my mother's mind and what she could accept from me. A "can-do" problem solver, I cobbled together weekly rituals through which I might pretend to be close to her and imaginatively pierce her thick veneer.

The valedictorian of her high school and college, my mother kept the yearbooks documenting her many past achievements stacked on the living-room bookshelves. Once a week I pulled all the books down off the shelves and laid them neatly in front of me. Now I was ready. Turning the pages one at a time, and always starting from the beginning, I discovered and rediscovered my mother's image in the group shots of clubs and associations. Held back till the very end of my devotional sessions was the final black-and-white glossy: a full-page portrait from the University of Toledo, her glorious face and hopeful expression gently tilted upward, revealing a slight smile. With her lips apart just a bit, she exposed her crooked front tooth, and I imagined she was about to laugh; a laugh that was meant for me. The caption: "Margery Bloor Wenner: Brains and Beauty." It packed a wallop every time.

Friday evenings—after she had concluded her week of teaching Latin to high school students—provided a few minutes of my mother's golden solo attention while I received my weekly hair shampooing. She would lift my tiny body and set me onto my back right on top of the kitchen counter, my head draped deep into the kitchen sink. Hair moistened, I held my breath, preparing myself for a rough and vigorous scrubbing as her long red nails dug deeply into my scalp. In my captive, supine position, I was tacitly given permission for just those few minutes to gaze at her, *examine* her intensely, and not look away. Shampoo burned the eyes in those days, so I had about a minute before the stinging set in. Then, succumbing to the pain, I reluctantly closed my eyes and blindly felt her hands roughly flutter over my head. The ritual hurt and burned, but I took it without a whimper.

Occasionally on Sunday mornings, with the Hoover safely wedged between us, I slacked off and let myself hope and imagine that she felt what *I* felt as I lay on the carpet and wallowed amid Isolde's words through Kirsten's voice. But that was all in my naive imagination. She dodged her young daughter's body, occasionally sucking a few strands of my hair into the Hoover, which did push a yelp out of me. With no apology, she aimed the Hoover in the other direction, bringing about mixed emotions. I wanted her to see me, even if it hurt. But she was simply cleaning the rug. Chagrined, I saw my error and righteously banished her to a spot in the background chorus, blending harmoniously with her Hoover. Her psychic whipping umbilical cord receded, just a coiled-up prop to be thrown offstage. Kirsten retook center stage, planting her feet squarely at the threshold of my ears and young life. *Kirsten* was my mother.

As I bode my time throughout the very long week while I waited for shampoo, heavy picture books, and Kirsten on Sunday mornings, a gauzy gray cloud washed over me. I was born a pint-size Sartre, my life's purpose the unanswerable question. This quandary, which I did not understand let alone want to face, demanded frequent relief. Sleep became the stopgap I could reach for, perhaps control, and I slept hard, often, like a dead dog. Not, however, to achieve the usual sense of relief after a long and tiring day; rather, when I slept, I could mentally tuck myself up on a very high shelf. For a time, my brain unraveled and relaxed, temporarily deadened to all troubling ideas and perceived slights. Midday, or at any time at all, I crawled unnoticed into my bed.

Everyone sleeps, but not everyone could use music the way I did. If sleep was an unconscious draft of lifesaving elixir, music was its waking counterpart: both offered me a way to forget my wearying existential dilemma and to shove aside the need for an answer, or for my mother. Wafting between one and the other, I could pry my eyes open for another day.

Behind

The principal flutist sits to your right; to your left, the second oboist. While playing, you sense their bodies shift to take a collective breath as the front row of the wind section performs a tutti passage. The string section fans out before you: violins, violas, cellos, and basses. But the musicians behind you are as good as invisible: the clarinets, the bassoons, the brass, and the percussionists.

A languid duet, played as a unison solo during the slow movement of a Schumann symphony, brings you in touch with the unseen principal clarinetist. He's a friend and musical colleague of many years, with whom you've shared the joy of the birth of his kids and the sadness of his subsequent divorce. And because of this close personal relationship, your inner eye is attuned to his musical life and particularly his artistic gestures during performance.

As the solo begins, you can't distinguish his sound from yours. At first, it's unnerving. Your sounds are meshed, creating a new composite sound, and for several seconds you doubt you're actually taking part at all. The intonation has no telltale beats, indicating pitch discrepancy—in short, it is perfect. Phrasing inflections ebb and flow as one. As you lose yourself in time, for-getting that you're performing for an audience, the music seems to play itself: effortless, the oboe weightless in your hands. Yet all the while, you sense a pressure on the back of your head: the clarinetist's eyes boring a hole into your skull.

At the end of the solo the full orchestra joins in again, to con-clude the movement.

It was intimate; you feel slightly embarrassed and carry this memory and sensation with you for many years. It has rarely been duplicated. Transformation within the shifting universe of music is singular and dear, like a newborn with flexing fists.

Proud

"IF YOU DON'T practice, you won't like it."

Mr. Proud repeated this gentle declarative warning often, and I was inclined to take him at his word. I was his somewhat dour fourth-grade music student; he, my deadpan first music teacher—and neither of us seemed to have much to smile about. The serious nine-year-old girl and the no-nonsense grown-up quickly developed an easy simpatico.

When Mr. Proud demonstrated the flute, clarinet, and trumpet at the beginning of the school year, my eyes widened with recognition—a few puzzle pieces had just snapped together before me. Up until that moment, music was largely intuitive for me, but now the heavens ripped open as I connected the sounds echoing in the classroom with the orchestra that was so familiar to me on Sunday mornings. But I had to quickly select what was to be my personal steed. The trumpet was just too blaring; the clarinet too honking, with a spreading-out wheeze. I easily chose the flute because its sweet, open quality most resembled Kirsten's burnished, silvery voice.

In the first lesson Mr. Proud taught the flute class how to blow into, or over, the mouthpiece of the flute. The room quickly filled with what sounded like children blowing over the tops of Coke bottles. Disoriented from the cacophony, I separated myself from my classmates, faced the corner of the room, and practiced the exercise for several minutes. A strong hand on my shoulder broke my concentration. Startled, I turned around and met Mr. Proud's intense brown eyes.

"Why are you standing in the corner?"

"I don't know.... I can't stand all the crazy noise."

"Neither can I. Okay. Show me what you can do."

I scrutinized his impassive face for a few seconds and then gave him four very long and steady hoots, in succession.

"Good."

He must have recognized the musically starved child before him. I was promptly sent home with a fingering chart, and in one week I managed to learn all twelve notes of the scale. Mr. Proud looked at me inquisitively in the second lesson: I could actually play the thing, after a fashion, and I could name all the notes to boot.

"Marcia, how did you learn all this in one week? Did you have help? Have you played another instrument?"

"No. But I know Kirsten."

"Who's Kirsten?"

"She's the lady who sings Isolde's song in the Wagner."

"You mean the composer Richard Wagner? How do you know about that?"

"She sings on Sunday mornings with the Hoover."

My cryptic explanation surely baffled him, but he left it alone.

As the school year progressed, whatever he asked me to prepare, I would return having mastered the assignment. His comment never varied.

"Good."

Nothing more.

On a very subtle level, he was teaching me something profound, a concept that many never feel comfortable with. Mr. Proud showed me that *I* would be the arbiter of how "good" I was. That was a huge chunk of adult to be laid right at my small feet.

The big event under Mr. Proud's yearlong fourth-grade tutelage was my performance of "Greensleeves" over the radio in Pittsfield, Massachusetts. Mr. Proud met me at the Pittsfield library, where I sat patiently with my flute in my lap. Stage—or radio—fright quickly set in. My heart pounded so hard I could feel the blood pulsing on my scalp, even out through my eyeballs. Slowly I got myself under control by closing my eyes and pretending to be asleep. Gradually my heart slowed down to an ordinary pace, and my sweaty palms dried up. And finally, saliva returned to my parched mouth.

When Mr. Proud gently shook me awake, my eyes found the head of the microphone looming large in front of me. An old lady pointed to me and screamed in a whisper:

"Okay, play *NOW!*"

I blasted out "Greensleeves" to beat the band.

Years later, when I was hired to teach smart and talented college kids at Columbia University (who were actually there for other reasons, like public policy and rocket science), I would echo Mr. Proud's gentle warning: "If you don't practice, you won't like it." They had terrifyingly full schedules, yet they still wanted to continue playing through their college years. My students initially tried to cram their practicing into one or two days before the lesson. There are no shortcuts, and I urged them to practice every day, even for just fifteen minutes, because sustainable progress comes from a dogged routine. Mr. Proud remained a heroic and steady beacon throughout my life by imparting one simple gift: the early understanding that anything challenging is only truly loved when engaged in every day. The getting-better part is the gravy.

Mr. Proud would leave at the end of the school year in the mid-1960s to become a New York State organic farmer.

"Marcia, I won't be back to teach you next year."

"Why not?"

"I'm going to farm organic vegetables in New York State."

"Why?"

"Because it's what I really want to do."

"Don't you really want to teach me?"

"Yes, but I'll be happier if I do this farming. Can you understand that?"

"Which vegetables will you grow?"

"Carrots and beets. Things like that."

"What's a beats?"

"It's a red vegetable."

"But who'll teach me my flute?"

Having no idea what an organic farmer was, I was understandably concerned for him. What organs was he talking about? The heart, kidneys, liver? It sounded dreadful, really.

As weeks passed, the end of the year closed in, looming ominously—and I was still optimistic that I might actually have some have sway over Mr. Proud's decision. At nine years old I had unwittingly had my first experience with someone who was a true pedagogue. The word comes from the Greek, meaning literally "to lead the child." To me it was simple: if he left, I might die. Death seemed an appropriate fear, because the future was dire. Surely he knew this.

I tried again.

"Do you really have to go do that farming thing?"

"Yes, it's all set up. It's like a new job."

"But why can't you stay here at your old job?"

"Marcia, remember I told you that this is something I *really* want to do."

"But I *really* want you to stay, 'cause if you go"—I let my fears seep out, and the tears started—"no one'll come to teach me my flute."

"The school will hire a new teacher."

"But *who* will it be?"

"I don't know, but the school will arrange it."

"But what if he *doesn't* come?"

"Someone *will* come. Just keep practicing. Every day. Like we talked about. Okay? You'll be fine."

We went over the same territory countless times toward the end of the school year, and he patiently repeated his assurances. Throughout the endless summer, I remained morose and unconvinced.

The next year we did indeed have a new music teacher, whose first name was Morris. Morris encouraged us fifth graders to call him, well, Morris. He had a comb-over, which I learned the name for only years later. (Oh, that's what he was doing! He was *bald!*) Cast with a certain élan, his gestures were flamboyant and exaggerated. Morris was as far from Mr. Proud as could be imagined.

At the first lesson of the school year, he dramatically whipped out some sheet music. "Greensleeves" had been in Method Book

1. Apparently Method Book 2 was not in my future. Instead, we learned the theme music to the movie *Peyton Place* and the theme song to a new TV soap opera called *Days of Our Lives*. Morris was dedicated to instilling in his students a healthy appreciation for the popular culture of the day. I remained wary.

Wild and unusual, Morris's peculiar mannerisms were hard to ignore, and over time I sensed he needed to be tamed, reined in, and perhaps tamped down a bit. So I became brave.

"Morris, I was wondering if we could learn some classical songs."

"Sure. Like what? Something like 'Moon River'? Give me an example."

"Well, what about Wagner?"

"Who?"

"Wagner…you know, *classical*."

"I don't know any Wagner.…I know *Jim* Wagner down at the car dealership, but I don't think he writes songs. We'll learn 'Moon River'—*that's* a classic."

I realize now that Morris was the Pittsfield equivalent of a club-date musician. Popular music. Maybe even jazz! He talked to me as if we were buddies on the bandstand sharing a slightly off-color joke. He might as well have been smoking a cigar.

Morris's loopy personality grew on me, especially since he did know how to play the flute and taught me well. I progressed steadily, but my secret yearning for Mr. Proud still tugged, and I imagined he might pop up one day, listen to me play, and be proud.

Pointe

Plinkety-plinkety-plink. Chunk-cachunk-cachunk. Bam-bam-wham. Whap! *That would be a waltz. From where you sit in the pit at City Center in New York City, you can't see what's going on, but you can hear it all through the floor of the stage, right above your head. This isn't going very well, you think to yourself. It's the first rehearsal for* Giselle, *and it sounds damned ugly—a cacophony of elephants galumphing above you, supposedly in unison. And they're not with the music. Ever.*

Dancing en pointe *is a noisy business. You can't imagine there is any semblance of synchronization up there. It's an aural freak show of pounding and banging and stutter-stepping. What kind of a company is this, anyway? They're supposed to be world-renowned stars of the ballet world. Why did you accept this gig? Money, of course.*

But later in the day you're able to slip out of the pit and into a theater seat during a ballet you're not playing in, and you begin to see what all the noise is about. The beauty is simply astonishing. Tutus floating with ivory tulle, buoying the body, as if in slow motion with every movement. Sixty arms gracefully arch, and then, precisely on beat 3, thirty fingers move an inch, all in a perfect communal gesture. Women's necks crane, suggesting swans on an imagined, almost frozen, glacial lake. Men lovingly grip their partners' middles and lift them to a heaven you can only dream of. Bodies meld like mercury— shifting from side to side and up and down—fluid, yet at that cusp of almost solid. You say a quiet mea culpa for doubting what you did not understand. Sixty toe shoes land on the floor of the stage, all within about one second of each other. But those sounds are just the toes. So much more is an attuned alignment from someone's God. Throughout the Dance Theatre of Harlem season, you fall in love with those clunks *and* plunks *and* whams, *because those sounds are supporting thirty artists who are balanced in multitudinous ways—unimaginable to the once blind and faithless oboist beneath their feet.*

Oboe

I WAS GAWKY at twelve, and certainly odd, but nothing prepared me for the onslaught of hideous teenage physical and psychic angst that blasted my way the first day in seventh grade at my new school. As I looked around, the concert-band room appeared to hold the most egregious offenders, boys with peach fuzz on their lips and girls who sported pointy bras. Everyone was unreasonably tall, embarrassingly spindly, and gravely ancient.

The September weather was still warm and muggy, and I'd perspired badly through the wool sweater my mother insisted I wear. Putrid body odors undulated from those around me, but I realized to my dismay that I was a full-fledged contributor, too! And to top it off, foul, fetid breath emerged from the trumpet players seated directly behind me as the band began to warm up. I could barely cough enough air into my lungs to play the flute.

But so much more was terribly amiss. Shortly into the band's warm-up scales, I saw that effluent oozing from pubescent and ripe teenagers alike was the least of my problems. The out-of-tune major scales, sounding like clusters of minor seconds, assaulted me as if on a grand moral scale. Mr. Fulginiti, our band director, put us through our virgin paces, showcasing the group's awful pitch and nonexistent rhythm. I took a chance in between the tone-row clusters to peek down my row to the right and to the left. All I saw were flute players, with breasts, no less—there must have been at least twenty of us. Now I was just one in a cast of thousands.

I went limp, defeated, wanting to jump up and run out of school, back to my living-room carpet, where Kirsten was waiting; or to my bed, where a solid nap would surely stamp out the disastrous future ahead of me. All it took was twenty voluptuous flute players and the smelly trumpet players who kept ogling them, with every single one producing noises from hell, for life to splatter on the ground before me.

As the period ended, I could feel tears prickling. I tugged at the three joints of my flute, yanking the awful thing apart. Just then Mr. Fulginiti hushed the crowded band room and held up a slender black instrument.

"I need a volunteer to play this. We only need one."

My hand shot up. Actually, I stood up, ensuring I would be taller than anyone else's hand, just in case I had challengers. In that split second I understood that, while I wanted to fit in, I needed to stand out. This lone instrument just might be my ticket out of Faust's band from the underworld. I didn't care that I had no idea what it was or even what it sounded like. I raced up to Mr. Fulginiti, and he handed over the instrument with its case and a few plastic reeds.

"What's your name?"

"Marcia Butler."

"Okay, Miss Butler, let's see what you can do with this. Stop by my office at the end of the day."

He called it an oboe. We were sitting opposite each other in his tiny, cramped office, our knees almost touching.

"How do I put it together?"

"Well, before we get into that, why don't you play the flute for me? The oboe is a very challenging instrument, and I want to be sure this is a good fit for you."

I played my best pieces for him, including "Moon River."

Mr. Fulginiti was quiet for a few minutes, nodding his head without speaking. My head sunk into my shoulders; I wasn't good enough.

"We might have a problem here."

"What's wrong?"

"You play extremely well; too well, actually."

"What do you mean *too* well?"

"No, no. Sorry. Not too well for you, but too well for *me*. I can hear that you're very gifted, and there's just no one around here who can teach you the oboe to the level I anticipate you'll need. Let me think about this for a minute."

I sat quietly. Still stinging from the morning band session, I wasn't even sure I wanted to play the flute, let alone this oboe. Life was simpler with just my Kirsten—and she didn't have breasts, at least as far as I knew.

"Tell you what. I can start you off, and we'll see where it goes from there."

"Can you play it?"

"No. I play the clarinet. But I'll learn it along with you."

I relaxed my shoulders, and my head popped up from its retracted position. For the first time during that first day of school, I gave a doubtful smile.

"Really?"

"Don't worry, Miss Butler. We'll work this out. You can come to my house and I'll give you lessons. Do you have any questions?"

"How do you pronounce your name?"

He was a gently gregarious, roly-poly Italian man, married but childless, so different from the dour Mr. Proud and the outlandish Morris. His name, initially an odd rough object I had to roll my teeth and tongue around to master, quickly smoothed down like rocks in a streambed. Mr. Fulginiti's teaching style was relaxed, and I quickly forgot that he was making it up as I progressed. Over the next two years we grew to love the oboe, side by side.

Once I could get around on the oboe, having learned the fingerings, Mr. Fulginiti stopped trying to play it himself and began to just teach me music through fundamentals, demonstrating occasionally on the clarinet. A flat line became an arc, with a soft beginning, growing to a fat middle, and diminishing to a whispered end. Notes could be held out (legato); or very short (staccato). An interval of two notes had to be perfectly in tune so that a potential phrase could grow from it. He focused on technical concepts, but always in service to music. We broke the melodies down and then, once each point was mastered, rebuilt them. Mr. Fulginiti had an odd character combination of determined and maniacal whimsy—kind of the "best of" Mr. Proud and Morris. And somehow we fit.

A bonus was his love of opera, particularly Puccini, which always seemed to be playing when I entered his home for my weekly lesson. The beginning of *La Bohème*, whose first twenty minutes run like the blazes, left me breathless. Puccini expertly wove those snippets of lyrical phrases through a rapid-fire orchestral backdrop. I imagined the singers gasping to keep up.

Mr. Fulginiti always reserved the last fifteen minutes of my lesson for listening to the likes of *La Bohème* and *Madama Butterfly*, and I left each session gratefully exhilarated by the dizzying possibilities of music. Yet my living-room carpet still beckoned when I returned home, and I dove deep into my honey of a diva: to my Kirsten. Terra firma. Land ho!

Saturday morning oboe lessons posed a hurdle for my parents, not only because Mr. Fulginiti lived thirty minutes away but also because my mother couldn't help with this weekly driving chore. Left-hand turns were not in her repertoire of skills. For some reason, she could only make a right-hand turn in our car, which led to looping, long trips wherever she went. For expediency's sake, my father became house chauffeur, but agreements had to be worked out first. He wanted to meet this Italian guy who had suspiciously offered to teach me at no charge.

An affable man to neighbors and strangers, my father was well built and handsome in a Waspy, steely-blue-eyed, Chiclet-toothed, Wonder Bread kind of way. But public persona aside, he had neither the warmth nor the flexible latitude of understanding necessary for children and their peculiarities. He was not quick to smile. But when he did, it appeared as a rigid-lipped slash across the face. I didn't trust him or his grim grin and worried that just because he could, he would undermine my agreement with Mr. Fulginiti.

We drove to the first scheduled lesson. As we pulled into the driveway, the front door swung open; Mr. F. beckoned to my father, all smiles and goodwill. My father entered the house, frowning and sour, obviously prepared to reject a "too good to be true" proposition. I waited in the car. Ten minutes, fifteen minutes, on to thirty minutes. And with each passing second my future receded back onto the far horizon as I stared straight ahead out the windshield of the car. That future was still a mental smear of something that had not yet even occurred to me. But it was there. And the possibility of that unknowable something was in my father's tight fist as he negotiated with Mr. Fulginiti inside a house I wanted very much to enter.

The door finally reopened, and my father emerged with his rigid smile stamped above his chin, while Mr. F. simply looked at me, ashen-faced.

"Come on in, Marcia. Let's get started."

A deal had been struck behind Mr. Fulginiti's front door: my father agreed to drive me to my oboe lesson, thirty minutes away, every Saturday morning. Not a cent changed hands between them. But I would pay.

Tit for Tat

MY FATHER AND I floated around the house, eyeing each other from a distinct distance. Our cautious détente was set in motion very early, my father the skilled raptor, me the baby mouse. Our truce, always on view, was easy and limpid. I lazed on his lap in our Pittsfield living room, at first naive to what would become my important role. An easier mark could not have been found. Still, there were many negotiations along the way yet to be ironed and flattened out.

I sucked my thumb incessantly and furiously, years past the age when children usually give up such soothing habits. At any given moment, one thumb or the other was wedged in my mouth, sodden and badly wrinkled. Shaming was my father's aim, and brutalizing barbs were his weapons.

"Get that thumb out of your mouth right now! You're much too old for that stuff and you *know* it. If I see you suck that thumb once more, I'll just sit right down next to you and suck mine along with you. I'm warning you. You'll never get rid of me. And get *that rag* off your face or I'll burn it!"

That rag was my beloved and filthy undershirt, secretly known as Undy. It wasn't just the egregiously wrinkled, sopping-wet thumb that bugged my father but also its indicted co-conspirator, my smelly undershirt. I liked to keep it near my cheek while I sucked, so I could inhale its wonderfully used odor. This tandem comfort seemed to soothe my titrating needs.

He threw down many gauntlets over the years, and I never knew when they might surface and grab me with pincers. My lifelong habits felt impossible to crack, and he knew it. In public and at home, he dug into me without warning.

One day, returning from one of my lessons, my father and I stopped off at a local bakery to pick up some rolls and brownies. Standing in line for the checkout, I was sucking and sniffing and daydreaming, clearly unaware that my thumb was front and center and Undy had made its cameo appearance for all to see.

He screeched a stage whisper that could have been heard in the balcony of Carnegie Hall.

"*Marcia*. That thumb. Out. That rag. Gone."

I quickly dropped my hands.

"Dad, I was thinking."

"Don't think. Just get that thumb out of your—"

"I know, I know. I *did*. But I wanted to ask you…"

Under duress, my thumbs always seemed to levitate to my mouth, as if a master puppeteer were controlling my digits.

"Thumb. Out. Rag. Gone. NOW."

People standing in the long line began to look the other way or up at the ceiling. Anywhere but at the uncomfortable father-daughter scene unfolding before them. I started my own urgent stage whisper, just to save some face.

"Dad, I have an idea.… What would you think—"

"Why are you whispering? Speak UP, for goodness' sake. I

can't *hear* you when you talk with your thumb in your mouth while facing the floor, you know."

My thumb had popped back in. Those thumbs really *did* seem to have a life of their own.

"I know, but just listen for a minute...."

We had reached the cashier, and my father was pulling out his wallet to pay while I continued my bargaining efforts. In one fleet gesture, he swiveled around, planted his face three inches from mine, and bellowed.

"WHAT?!"

The cashier stopped midmotion; the entire bakery—silent. An ocean roared in my head, filling a quiet vacuum as I tried to offer a solution that might resolve all our problems. Or at least one of them.

"Okay, so what if I stopped sucking my thumb. But...I-kept-Undy?"

The last three words ran unbroken out of my mouth, perhaps a potential new word in the Queen's English. A puzzled look emerged on the cashier's face, surely uncertain as to what an "Ikeptundy" was.

With his face still pinned close to mine, my father's dead, blue-eyed stare burned into my pupils. My mother hated it when I looked at her. But an unbroken gaze was required with my father. That's just the way it was; you had to go through with it. *His* way. And always the eyes.

"That sounds fair."

Done. It was surprisingly easy. We left the store in silence as I imagined the eyes of the bakery patrons burning a hole in the back of my head.

My father was unpredictable; even conventions of politeness

were brushed aside. Trying to cobble together a daily plan of action with him was often hit or miss. But as I grew older, I began to understand a bit more how he viewed the world. If I sacrificed, something in turn might be delivered. Also known as tit for tat.

The musical love of my father's life was the pop singer Vikki Carr, his girlfriend from the suitable distance of an LP. During occasional moments of reverie, he plunked himself on the corner club chair in the living room and listened to Vikki's albums as she sang the words: "Oh dear God / It must be him / It must be him." Even as a small girl, I could tell Vikki was a woman on the brink—of what, I couldn't fathom. But before too long I actually began to appreciate Vikki, too. She really *could* sing and had that "on the brink" wobbling vibrato in her voice that made for wonderful tension. Though much less refined than Kirsten, Vikki definitely laid her vocal chops on the poker table.

But this musical alliance between Vikki and my father did not sit well with my mother. She *detested* Vikki Carr. In fact, music was a wonder of nature my mother had trouble connecting to in general—Wagner on Sunday mornings the inexplicable oddity. Our home was devoid of melody, with the exception of a burgeoning oboist. To keep the peace with her, my father did his own little tit-for-tat dance and began to use headphones. Vikki's wobble now seeped out from the cans.

He beckoned to me. What little girl could resist those outstretched arms and *not* walk gingerly across the living room to cozy up on her daddy's lap? He stretched the headphone strap to the limit, and we each took an ear.

In my selective memory, there was *that day,* then the dulled sepia blur of what felt like every single minute after. I squirmed uncomfortably in his lap, as I tried to figure out what I was feeling. My father took hold of my shoulders to still me. He looked into my sweet little-girl blue eyes with his steel-trap blue raptor eyes.

"Are you comfortable?" he asked.

The very first word I learned to read in the first grade was *balloon*. Balloons always held my careful attention: I would track them as they floated up and finally disappeared past the clouds. I also clearly remember the bright, stinging sensation of snowflakes when they first touched my cheeks and eyelashes. Children will flatten their faces to the sky, anticipating that first flake of winter for the rest of their childhoods. Naming the color red is another early childhood rite of passage. Red is not orange or scarlet, but only red.

A child ticks off these discoveries with her small hands, finger by finger. But where in my childhood journal of firsts would I inscribe *this* particular rite of passage? On the first page or the last? In the dedication or the acknowledgments?

Our eyes locked. My hands crimped into tightly balled fists. *Now* I was aware, and he *knew* I was aware. With a small, snapped nod of my head, our binding and sickening pact was sealed. I had already been performing an innocent's lap dance for years, but I had just connected the awful dots, and we were now in conscious collusion.

"Yes, Father. I'm comfortable. I'm fine."

"Good girl."

My father was my epic Wagnerian Wotan. I was his dutiful daughter Brünnhilde. In Richard Wagner's *Ring* cycle, a set of four operas lasting fifteen hours, Wotan rules over his kingdom, Valhalla, and all the gods and his family with the tightest of fists. Wotan has been ennobled by pacts set up by the gods and connives with everyone around him, including his faithful Brünnhilde, to ensure they do his bidding. Sanguine and easy, I was determined to do my own Wotan proud. I became the best little Brünnhilde this side of his Valhalla, a mythical place that would become my childhood prison.

It was so simple and yet unimaginably urgent: I needed him to drive me to my oboe lessons with Mr. Fulginiti, thirty minutes away by car. Brünnhilde sacrificed her childhood for something essential and lifesaving. Wotan gave up a few hours of his weekend.

We quickly settled into the routine. On Saturday mornings he drove me, sat in the car for the hour, and waited for me to learn how to play my oboe. We signed in blood, and I kept the count: one lap, two laps, maybe even three laps for one lesson. However many he wanted, I sat rigid—knowing, silent, and stricken—for the remainder of my time under his roof.

Kirsten sang:

In the wafting Universe of the World-Breath
Drown.

Speed

You do it because you can get away with it. That is, if everything lines up precisely and no one screws up. Booking a concert on a Sunday afternoon and an evening concert on the same day is nothing out of the ordinary for New York City freelancers. Except when the afternoon performance begins at 3:00 p.m. and the evening concert begins at 6:30 p.m.—and the concert venues are in different cities. Then things just might get interesting.

The afternoon concert in Stamford, Connecticut, will end at 5:15 p.m., leaving you about one hour to make your 6:30 p.m. downbeat in Alice Tully Hall at Lincoln Center. If there's no traffic and if the gods are with you, the car trip can come in at forty minutes flat. But there is another complication—the first piece on the program in Tully Hall is Rossini's overture to La Scala di Seta, *which has one of the most famous and devilishly difficult oboe solos in the orchestral repertoire. You will need steely nerves for what you pray is the perfect car ride and what you hope will be a memorable performance.*

Three other musicians have accepted both concerts as well, and the contractors who've hired for the two orchestras have

*been alerted to your risky road trip. They don't like it at all—
and you could be jeopardizing future work if you are late and
responsible for holding up the start of the evening concert. But
the urge to try to be literally everywhere, and play every concert,
takes over rational thinking. And you really want to play that
Rossini overture.*

*The Connecticut concert ends on time, at 5:16 p.m., and the
four of you pack up quickly and run to the car, which has been
strategically positioned in the parking lot for a fast exit. Then a
surprise wrinkle quickly develops once you get on the road. The
cellist, Brian, is driving, and as you head up the ramp to join
I-95 south, he pulls a bottle of Jim Beam from his jacket and
takes three long gulps. The excited chitchat in the car immediately ceases. You turn to him and say, "What the fuck, Brian?"
He looks at you with dead eyes and tells you, very calmly, that
he needs to be loose so he can drive fast. With that statement he
floors the gas pedal and begins to weave in and out of traffic at
ninety miles an hour.*

*You sit back and look straight ahead. You go inside yourself,
to that familiar flat and parched landscape where sensate danger is held at your brain barrier. No one talks, and the car
becomes as quiet as coffins waiting for bodies. You look at the
backseat just once to see four eyes slammed shut. With deep, regularly paced swigs of bourbon, Brian finishes off his bottle just
as you get to the 96th Street exit off the Henry Hudson Parkway.
Running red lights on Broadway, he pulls up to the Tully Hall
stage door to let you out, because he knows you have to run in
to warm up. The wheels squeal as he turns the corner to park in
the lot under Lincoln Center.*

That evening the concert isn't your best, but it's not the worst, either, and you don't remember much of the Rossini at all. Your big solo moments are over before you can allow yourself to un-wind and feel anything. Just like Brian, you are on automatic pilot—loose, feeling nothing—so you can speed to the conclu-sion of the concert.

Jinx

BEING A NEOPHYTE negotiator, I was terrified to tip the balance of my hard-earned peace between my father and myself, because his outstretched arms could reverberate with another energy. He had that pent-up, clock-block, Robert-De-Niro-playing-Jake-LaMotta anger, which he unleashed regularly onto my older sister, Jinx, her nickname. A few years apart in age, we were polar opposites in temperament, and tit for tat wasn't a game she bothered to play. Whether they were driven by her choice of boyfriends, staying out too late, running away from home, not cleaning her room, or just general sassiness toward my mother, my father's fists were out in front to meet her, clutching metal crops. I heard those whapping slaps from behind her bedroom door when my father had had enough and wanted to teach her the way he preferred: through force. Those awful sounds stabbed into my discerning ears and guts, and no matter what room in the house I sought for relief, I heard all of it.

A master of defiance, Jinx was irritating and a difficult sister to like. During those overheard battles I sat very still, silently raging—not against my father but against Jinx. Couldn't she simply negotiate an acceptable settlement with him, as I had? But she just wouldn't back down, and her answers were always a deafening *no*.

One very bad night I woke up, hearing banging downstairs. Racing to the top of the stairway, I looked down to see my father charging at Jinx like a heavyweight prizefighter. My view from the top showed only his broad back as he pushed her into the corner of the stair landing below. He cocked his right arm back and punched hard, almost putting her eye out. The right angle of those two walls joining on the stair landing held her solidly, at just the right position for his fist. That sound, fist on orbital bone, startled me—it sounded like a very thick stick not wanting to give way but finally snapping in two.

"You bitch."

He said those brutal words, too calmly. I didn't know what a bitch was, but I knew it must have been an awful thing to be. Crumpled into the corner, squatting on her haunches, her feet on the carpet, pigeon-toed to give her traction, she took it all without a struggle.

I stood back as Jinx ran up the stairs past me, straight into the bathroom. Suddenly there was no sound anywhere in the house, as if all living matter had been sucked out. My father was still on the landing, his arms braced against the wall, his head hanging down with his chin at his chest. I shifted my weight, hoping to just go back into my bedroom unnoticed, but he heard me. As he slowly turned around, our eyes met. He was expecting to see his obvious victim. Instead he saw the secret one.

"Bob?"

My mother was offstage, downstairs in the living room. Her voice dead calm, terse. My father snapped his head toward her as if surprised. Realizing she had witnessed this, too, I felt stomach bile come up, quickly. But I swallowed.

"Mom?"

"Go back to bed, honey."

We had always been a family of the fewest possible words, scraped clean.

Jinx's skin had been ripped open, leaving a searing red slash of bare pulp. She needed stitches, but my mother let it go, allowing the exposed flesh to slowly heal itself into a flat beige scar. My mother wouldn't or couldn't take the risk to intervene, perhaps working out her own peculiar standoff with my father.

I didn't cry that night. But somewhere there's a memory I can almost access: guttural sounds—sobs—terrible inhuman wails. I lay awake all night, plotting what I should do—ruminating on a Band-Aid to stretch across a rampant epidemic. The next morning I marched defiantly into school, walked up to my homeroom teacher, Mr. Firth, looked him in the eyes, and asked point-blank:

"Can you call the police on your own parents if they are beating up someone in your family?"

He didn't skip a beat.

"*Well*, it depends on the severity."

"What do you mean?"

"*Well*, if it were within an inch of the child's life, I would say yes. Anything other than that, it would depend."

"Depend on what?"

My eyes widened with a horrified internal reckoning. I really *got* it now: there would be no help. I was unprotected, marooned; hanging onto some kind of capsized sailboat while the spectators on shore watched through binoculars. My short exchange with Mr. Firth was the only time I risked exposing the hell inside my house. The way he shut me down felt like the final cutoff of a symphony, but minus the applause.

The brain is a marvelous organ, able to cleverly stratify the forces it can barely withstand. I know, in retrospect, that I appeared mildly vacant, almost concussed. I began to bear up. I took whatever came, yet I remained publicly palatable, albeit flattened out. As I conserved my internal grit, lists were made, stacks were straightened, plans were dreamed of, and rough edges were pounded down and rounded out. I was the strange one who blew the oboe and shunned a typical teenager's life, and adults and teachers seemed to give me the space I needed. I had a different kind of best friend, other kids would learn, and it wasn't a human being. I eschewed people for a stick of granadilla wood.

Day after day I listened and practiced. I absorbed and learned. I grew up under the cover of music's nonviolent and nonsexual realm. Kirsten continued to stand in as my understudy mother and helped me harmonize and orchestrate my atonal world. Nailing my head next to the stereo all day and night now, setting the needled arm on repeat, I remembered what Mr. Proud said.

You'll be fine. Just keep practicing. You'll be okay.

Shut Up

*You're onstage. You've nailed your part in the practice studio.
You have a great reed for the performance. The music on the program is familiar, like an old friend. What a great way to make
a living! You feel so very lucky.*

*Not that luck has much to do with it. You can't live unless
you practice the oboe every single day of the year. Year after year
after year. Because you know in the pit of your belly that something terrible will happen if you take even ONE. DAY. OFF. It
sounds strange and desperate. But why tempt the Fates? You'd
rather just keep doing it, exactly the same way.*

*Then you look up and see the guy standing on the podium and
begin to worry. For about thirty seconds before the concert starts,
you allow yourself a little mental rant. Why is this guy even up
there? He can't do his job even half as well as 99 percent of the musicians in the orchestra staring back at him. If he had to endure the
same scrutiny you do on a daily basis, he'd be digging ditches in
Detroit. Sure, he waves his arms around and looks good, at least
to the audience. But the orchestra knows that his movements don't
mean much at all, because they don't articulate his interpretation
of the music. That's his job, by the way: interpreting the music.*

You bring the reed close to your lips: fifteen seconds now. You think back to the four days of rehearsals prior to this concert. Every time he needed to give instruction, he actually stopped the orchestra to talk about it. Every time he had a note to an individual player, he had to silence the orchestra and verbalize his thought. And you want to scream, "Shut up! Just show us. Use the baton or your arms or your hands or even tell us with your eyes! Because if you can't show us in a nonverbal way during the rehearsals, how the hell are you going to do it in the performance?"

You think, for instance, what if you had to stop playing the oboe and explain verbally what you meant every time you played a phrase in a particular way? Well, first, you physically couldn't—the instrument is in your mouth. And second, you'd be fired on the spot or at the very least never hired again. You have to be a good enough player to communicate your musical intention through playing. Sounds reasonable, right? Not for that guy standing in front of you.

Yes. Year after year after year. No matter where you are in the world, you pull that oboe out of the case and practice. Just to keep the mouth flexible and supple and strong and familiar. Just to keep the fingers moving. Just to be crystal clear about your musical intention when playing. Just to be certain that you've done your very best. Just to keep on living.

The Move

I was in total control of my tenterhooks life. If worries bubbled up, I'd practice, sleep, or put a record on the stereo. Or if the trusted balancing act felt askew, I'd just go to my father to even things out. I could always put a few lap visits in the bank for a rainy day. Or so I thought.

My father received a promotion within General Electric, his lifelong employer, and was transferred to the New York City Lexington Avenue office. We bought a house in St. James, Long Island, and prepared to move the summer before I entered the ninth grade.

Jinx would not be joining us. The epic one-way battles between her and my father's fists had continued to escalate in frequency and intensity. Flagging from the strain, my parents chose an action that was surely baffling and inconceivable to most: they relinquished their legal parental rights to their daughter. The mighty Commonwealth of Massachusetts stepped in and sent Jinx to a reform school, where she was housed for a year with all manner of recalcitrant girls. I will never know if this decision was easily made.

This punitive warehouse for bad girls was the worst of places:

grim, dirty, and for the most part nonrehabilitative. Some girls had committed serious crimes, and most had very rough backgrounds. And then there was Jinx. I didn't like my sister much— we had nothing in common and virtually no sisterly camaraderie. Indeed, we barely spoke. But the ease with which she was deposited into this place felt like a nasty sleight of hand, because I was not told about their decision until just a day or two before she left.

With this underpinning of uncertainty in the air, I was on guard. Like any young girl, I was scared to death to go to a new town and a new school, but not for the reasons you'd imagine. I had few attachments and none that were deep. Losing the bond of girlhood friendships was not a particular worry. My more immediate concern centered on my potential inability to resurrect my carefully crafted eccentric life.

With Jinx out of the way, the summer was a blur of packing and boxes. My mother, if at all possible, seemed ever more distant. By contrast, my father exuded an almost jocular pretense. The frenetic activity heightened my sense of dread, destabilizing my orbit. I worried that my bargaining chips would disappear. Even *that* was a concern.

I had a shameful secret that I allowed myself to acknowledge only when I was feeling very fragile and sad. This secret helped soothe me and cope with what I understood would most likely be a terrible new life. I was actually thankful that Jinx was not coming with us. *Hallelujah*. Finally, there might be some version of peace in our house. I wouldn't have to think about her defiance. What booze she was drinking. What classes she was cutting. And *finally*, I might no longer be a captive audience, a listening witness to the beatings that raged mostly behind bedroom doors. In a quiet house, my *oboe* would be the loudest sound.

Having said a stoic good-bye to Mr. Fulginiti, I began the ninth grade in St. James, where so many things were new, the least of which was a newfangled teacher who actually *played* the oboe. Lessons with Mr. Kemp, now more than an hour away, were improved, with a new attention to technical depth. I also began to learn the art of reed making. With these higher stakes, I was grateful that one old agreement remained ironclad—Wotan and I still tangoed. I sat, and he drove. The familiar and comforting stability of my father's urge deflected the many new unsettling shifts in our house.

Pucci

As I SPENT more time in the car with my father, my mother's left-turn aversions reared up anew with frightening roads like the Long Island Expressway and the Northern State Parkway snaking their way dangerously close to our house. This dauntingly complex tangle of highway systems nudged her into a secret spending habit called catalogs. The packages arrived from mysterious places like Lord & Taylor and B. Altman, and up they went into her bedroom. One of the dresses that came via the post was a black-and-white number with a loud Pucci-like print, fashionable in the '60s. It was floor-length with a tight waist and a tasteful flare at the bottom. The silhouette was decidedly Grecian. Think Mrs. Robinson out at the pool, at night, perhaps with Benjamin.

That black-and-white dress! On nights she and my father attended neighborhood parties, it transformed my mother into the hopeful young woman I had worshipped in her college yearbook: *Margery Bloor Wenner: Brains and Beauty.* As they prepared to leave for the evening, she floated around the living room swathed in the dress, loose-lipped, already filled to the brim with whiskey sours and smelling of the Shalimar perfume I begged her to let me use.

"Mom, I love that perfume. Can I wear it to school tomorrow?"

"No, honey, it's too grown-up for you."

"But Joette Delia wears it to school. *Her* mother lets her."

"Well, Joette Delia's mother is an idiot. *Honestly.*"

Living on Long Island, and in closer proximity to New York City, offered me more places to play music. The St. James ladies' club, apparently always on the lookout for fresh talent, called one day and encouraged me to audition for a concerto competition that was being held by the Suffolk Symphony, a local professional orchestra. Word had spread quickly about my talent; it was unusual for an oboist to compete in a competition that usually drew pianists and violinists. One of the ladies' club members played the piano fairly well and offered to accompany me during the competition, and she also volunteered for the arduous job of picking me up and driving me to her house so we could rehearse.

These driving arrangements felt hushed and secret, and I don't recall one conversation with my mother about how I would get places. The kindness shown me in the area of getting *anywhere* was stunning. Cars simply appeared, and I was transported. People did not whisper. People did not gossip. But they *must* have known about my peculiar mother, and they were nonetheless very, very kind.

I won the competition. The next day that black-and-white dress appeared, spread out on my bed.

"Honey, this'll work for the concert."

"No, I can't wear that dress.... It's not right.... Not for a concert."

"What do you mean? It's perfect, and we're just about the same size now. Try it on. You'll see."

"But Mom, it's not right for a *concert.*... It's too..."

I searched for the right word. *Sexy* was the right word. Instead I chose *glamorous*.

"*You* know what I mean. Glamorous."

"Just try it on."

Her voice turned flat. This felt important to me. She wouldn't let me spray myself with Shalimar; why this dress? I let it blow.

"Mother. I want my own dress. It's a special concert, and I *deserve* it."

Tilting her head up, eyes canted down, she looked my way with doubtfully raised eyebrows. Okay, maybe I didn't exactly *deserve* it, but I kept on, now with a more cloying affect.

"*Why* can't I have my own dress?"

Silence.

"Okay... just give me *one* reason."

"The one and *only* reason is that if it fits, and I think it will, there is no *good* reason to spend more money."

I knew what this was really about. If she relented and agreed to take me shopping, she'd have to either make left-hand turns or spend hours in the car avoiding them. God knows my father wouldn't do it. Our agreement didn't include that shopping clause. My mother was expedient, if nothing else.

"I *need* to wear my own dress!"

The words poured out. I ranted and raved and begged and pleaded. Finally I tried on the dress. Much to my chagrin, it fit like a glove.

"Honey. *Look*. It's *perfect* on you. There's absolutely no need to buy something new."

"This is *unfair!* I won't play the concert. I want my own special concert dress. Please. Please. *Please?* I'll pay for a new dress out of my Christmas money. I'll do whatever you and Dad want...."

With those words, my mother turned and walked out of the room.

What Dad wants.

My guts seized up and left me staggered, then rigid: my father liked that dress very much. He had complimented her in that dress just the week before. I was now in competition with my mother over a dress I hated. I didn't ask for *this* kind of audition.

What Dad wants.

I wore that dress for the concert. I inhabited my mother. I became her mystery. I filled out the bodice. I looked very grown-up. I got some glances. And I played very well.

A man approached me after the concert for an interview for the local newspaper and asked which music school I would be attending after high school. Somewhat nonplussed by this new idea, I gave a vague answer that must have been planted somewhere in my subconscious.

"Oh, one of the New York City music conservatories, I *imagine*."

Being dressed in a fake Pucci gown had heightened my sense of sophistication. The man chuckled.

"I *imagine* you will!"

The Lone Sock

ONE AFTERNOON MY mother returned home from teaching Latin classes at a junior high school a few towns away from St. James and trudged up the stairs. I stood at the top of the stair landing, anxiously waiting for her arrival home.

The bedroom behind me looked as if a hasty thief had trashed it, with all the closet doors open, hangers bald. My mother walked in and looked at me, perplexed. She couldn't quite glean the meaning of the empty space.

"What's this? What's going on in here?"

"She's gone."

"What do you mean? Where's Jinx?"

"She's *gone*. All her clothes are gone."

I opened an empty chest of drawers to press my point.

After spending almost one year in the girl slammer in Massachusetts, Jinx had eventually come home to St. James and our new house. She returned docile and pliant, her facade weathered and less assured, less quick to anger. Something massive and surely disturbing had to have shifted her demeanor so drastically—but once home, she refused to speak about it; not that anyone asked in more than a passing manner. As far as my parents were concerned, that meal was chewed and digested.

A suspicious calm had engulfed the house during the first weeks of her return. I listened carefully, on watch, waiting for a knockout fight. But it never came. When my sister entered a room, my father left. Her rumpled room was what remained of her brief homecoming.

Now, scanning the room, my mother seemed to be calculating her next move. A single knee sock lay on the floor, balled up, without a partner. Jinx's bed was stripped of the bedclothes, which lay in a pile in the corner of the room. The mattress was slightly offset from the box spring by about twelve inches, not evened up. I tried to put myself in Jinx's frame of mind— why take the sheets off? She never made her bed, let alone changed her own sheets. Perhaps some vestige from the reformatory, one of the many punitive rules she must have obeyed for a time.

Without a word, my mother pushed past me, walked down the long hallway to her bedroom, and closed the door. She no doubt drew the shades shut. I sat on the top step of the stairway, listening for movement; any sign to signal a plan of action, a gesture of concern, a single sob. Sleep rolled over me—hours later, my father came home, stepping past me on the stairs to join my mother in the bedroom. My head lolled on the wall opposite the stair banister. The single sock continued to creep into my semi-sleep. I was a girl who paired things up and would never leave a box spring askew on a bed. I surmised, as I dozed, that Jinx's escape must have stemmed from a catastrophic experience that would never be shared.

It was late—maybe eleven at night—before I reentered her denuded room. Jostling the mattress to even it up with the box spring, I scooped up the lone balled sock and threw it roughly in my trash basket. I slept.

What was going to be done? This time I was not as gleeful as when Jinx was shipped off a year before. This time, something was very different, and when I woke with a start the next morning, there was a fresh-cut reality enshrouding our house. My sister had behaved well and had toed the line. She changed her stance and had said *yes*. Yet still she fled.

She may have called a week later to assure my mother that she was okay. Safe. Of course she wasn't, but the assurances of a young, just barely seventeen-year-old girl were all my parents needed to absolve themselves. Perhaps they had concerns, but not enough to make a move to get her back. This daughter, the queen of *no,* was loose in New York City in 1969, probably saying *yes* to someone.

"But where *is* she?"

"We don't know, honey, but your father and I think this is for the best."

"But what will *happen* to her? Is she staying in a hotel? She doesn't even have any *friends* in the city."

"Honey. You just have to let it go. There's just nothing more to say on the subject."

She turned and left the room.

Let it go. Let her go. If they could let her go without a yelp, what would they do for me? An infinitesimal fissure ruptured my longing for my mother. Who could be safe from a mother who did not search for a newly docile and obedient runaway daughter? It didn't add up; the math was faulty. My sweet little-girl blue eyes became devious, slithering-sneaky snake eyes. A trickster was born.

The King

On tour with an orchestra, you're taking a busman's holiday; the only night off you've had in six days of back-to-back concerts. You manage to get the last ticket available for the Royal Concertgebouw Orchestra performing at the Concertgebouw in Amsterdam. Stepping into the empty box, you are surprised when Dutch people lean over and ask, "How did you manage the king's box?" Oddly, they know to speak English to you. But you have no idea—it was just the last ticket available for a sold-out concert. So you settle in for the program, feeling like a queen, resisting the temptation to wave to your Dutch dominion.

Those Dutch oboe players snap at it, crisply, all through the program. You don't sound like them at all, but you imagine that you could easily make a sound like this, just as you could imagine living in this human-scale city, full of relaxed bicycle riders. Earlier in the day, you prayed for the young children hanging off the back of bikes as their mothers, pedaling in front, held loose and swinging bags of groceries, weaving in and out of traffic. You could even imagine being loved by a Dutchman, maybe even the king of Holland! These men of Flanders might ride bikes recklessly, be direct and to the point, and have smiling eyes. But they also may have straight and assured mouths, just like the Dutch oboists. Just like you.

But this orchestra sheds all vestiges of its well-bred, seventeenth-century elite Dutch manner for the last piece on the program: Dmitry Shostakovich's Fifth Symphony—the old warhorse that you played when you were in high school. The last movement is arranged for symphonic band and is a staple in all high schools with good music programs. Tonight, RCO heaves it at you, throttling you and driving it home.

During the relentless last movement your eyes gradually land on the timpanist, who is positioned at the back of the orchestra and directly in front of the conductor. The sound of his pounding mallets, at the end of his swinging Fred Astaire arms, catapults over the conductor's head and lands in your lap, in the king's box, in Amsterdam.

The timpanist and the conductor start to play their game with each other, and you wonder, who is in control here? This guy, the Dutch timpanist, is pummeling his story, one stroke at a time. The Italian conductor wants to hear it, feel it, be led by it, and graciously steps aside, allowing the beating to hold the night.

My God. Maybe it's the king's box. Maybe it's Rembrandt's house, which you saw earlier in the day, or the slightly fetid smell of a canal that wafts through the open window in your hotel room. But maybe it is just that damned drummer and that unconventional conductor who are now complicit, acting as one heavenly, dual person—causing you to levitate off your seat. You are thrilled by the pulse; by the easy sway of two people agreeing to be in service to music's greatness. And you are a queen: hearing, seeing, feeling, bearing witness to something extraordinary—something that will never occur again: that night in Amsterdam when Shostakovich was channeled from the dead and came alive, vibrating at the end of the timpanist's mallets, through a conductor's brain and directly into your heart.

Yes

WITH MY SISTER off to the squared and triangled streets of New York City, I raced unbridled into my plan. I was a talented oboist, certainly. But I also worked harder and practiced longer than seemed reasonable to anyone who observed me. With a highly developed, almost desperate sense of discipline (three hours of practicing a day was the norm) and with the guidance of my teacher, Mr. Kemp, I became a small-town star throughout my high school years. The local newspapers wrote articles; the principal of my high school wrote a *poem* about me after I'd received a favorable review in a Rochester newspaper; I played in all the area youth orchestras. But doubts lingered: I had no idea if I was good enough to get into that music conservatory I'd nonchalantly alluded to.

And then there was money. The default position in our household was that we were continually on the brink of financial collapse, which I suspected was the reason my mother was so secretive about her catalog habits. I never knew what the truth was, but I was always afraid to ask.

The State University of New York at Stony Brook had opened in 1962, and it was to become the state's go-to university for science and math. I was assured they had a music department tucked somewhere behind the math buildings and science labs. Because we lived nearby, my parents prepared me for that deadening eventuality. My backup school was to be the Katharine Gibbs secretarial school.

With those plans well cemented and inevitable, I boldly began to gather together application materials for music conservatories. The packets arrived in the mail, in full view of my parents, but were never commented on. When it came time for the auditions, I boarded the Long Island Railroad and negotiated New York City on my own with my oboe tucked in my backpack. Girding myself for inevitable rejection, or if by some miracle I was accepted, the reality was, I would be unable to pay. Yet I just stuck my neck out regardless. Letting me go through the motions, my parents, I sensed, knew something I didn't: that this was all a terrible joke; that I was in a dark tunnel and I'd never get a glimpse of a faint beacon of light. Jinx's choice almost seemed a reasonable final solution: maybe I'd run away to New York City, too, and lay myself prostrate at the door of a music school.

Acceptances soon came in from the Manhattan School of Music and the Eastman School of Music. I'd played a terrible audition for the Juilliard School. Just an hour before I was scheduled to play, I'd witnessed a trumpet player friend, who'd also come to audition, get hit by a car near the underpass on 65th Street. I was so unnerved that my hands shook badly throughout the audition. The jurors said nothing; they released me with a kind "Thank you, dear," before I'd finished the first line of the Haydn Oboe Concerto. I wasn't surprised by the rejection letter. Scholarships were not forthcoming from Manhattan or Eastman, so, disappointed, I quietly tore up the acceptance letters and threw them in the garbage. I waited.

Then it happened. The only phone in the house was in the kitchen; when it rang, my mother always picked up. She listened for a long time, responding mostly in monosyllables. I knew it was about me, because she kept looking up at me while the person on the other line talked. My mother called out to my father.

"Bob, get in here. It's Mannes College calling for Marcia!"

She pushed the phone in my direction.

"They want to talk to you."

The head of the woodwinds department was on the other end of the line. He shared the news with me: I had been offered a four-year full scholarship to the Mannes College of Music in New York City as a recipient of the prestigious Helena Rubinstein grant. They would pay for four years of tuition. I would be attending a real music conservatory in New York City, beginning in the fall of 1973.

As I stood in the kitchen, trying to digest the enormity of the news, my stance unconsciously and incrementally modulated. With arms set across my chest, my foot began to instinctively tap to a rhythm only I could hear. I turned my back on my parents, discussing the details with the man from Mannes. Hanging up the phone after replying with a resounding "YES!" I took a few moments to wallow in that glorious gush of freshly infused plasma pushing through the clotted blood that had for so many years felt viscous, sluggish. I knew my parents had to yield to me now.

I swiveled around, facing them. They remained silent—chagrined, almost. My mother left the room with no words. My father and I stared each other down, and I silently dared him to say one word. We carefully considered each other—both of us feeling the weight of my childhood. After several long seconds he turned to the refrigerator, pulled out a soda, and retired to the living room to have a romp with Vikki through the headphones.

Small droplets of golden hope trickled into my veins. Wotan would now bend to his Brünnhilde, and I would turn *left*.

Kirsten sang:

Friends! Look!
Don't you feel and see it?
Do I alone hear this melody,
Which wonderfully and softly…
Invades me?

Mannes

FREEDOM. OR SO I thought. As an eighteen-year-old, I had difficulty shaking loose from my father's tightly harnessed halter. Even with the relief of the glorious fifty miles of physical distance from him. Or with the help of a made-up grace in my head, Kirsten, who'd gently steered me away from every looming precipice. Freedom didn't tell me which direction to take. East, west, up, or down: freedom didn't tell me which was the road best traveled or where easy and deep-trodden footsteps might show me the way. In the fall of 1973, I moved to New York City, panting hard, with my arms outstretched, palms open to the wind, to tightly grab whatever came my way.

The Mannes College of Music was located on the Upper East Side of Manhattan on East 74th Street. Henry Fonda's house flanked one side; we saw Yul Brynner's bald pate occasionally exit it. The composer Charles Ives had lived at one time across the street. Tony Curtis often strolled by, along with other well-heeled people of the day. Mannes did not have a dormitory, nor did any other music conservatory in New York City in the early 1970s. I had the free ride to school, but now I needed free digs.

The well-heeled doyenne of my new life was Mrs. S., a beautiful and sophisticated Grace Kelly–like woman of newly divorced means. She'd registered with the school, offering food and lodging to a student in exchange for child care. Beginning my first semester of college, I lived with Mrs. S. and her two kids, right across the street from Mannes. For a maid's room off the kitchen and board, all that was required of me was to care for her young son and daughter three mornings and three evenings a week. The rest of the time was technically mine—to practice the oboe, to attend my classes, and to try to become the artist I couldn't yet imagine. The registrar at Mannes, a nun in a former life and well versed on rules and rigor, helped me patch all my coursework around my duties for Mrs. S. It was, in theory, ideal: a rigid life where I knew what was expected; lists, schedules, organized time, hard work, and mummylike sleep was what I hoped for.

The very first day of classes, I realized I knew absolutely nothing. Less than zero, actually—or so it seemed at first glance. Like any person embarking on a vast field of study that had previously been a youthful, singular passion, I found actually pulling apart the molecules of music to be both breathtakingly effervescent and bewilderingly impossible. At times I was levitating; other days, I felt I was looking up from the bottom of a New York City manhole. Music theory, sight singing, dictation, music history, music analysis, twentieth-century survey, orchestra, chamber music, art history, Western literature, European history. Oboe lessons. That was my insurmountable first-semester curriculum, but I trudged up those stairs, just off Mannes's walnut-paneled lobby, every day.

The bright, glowing aura surrounding the school was the faculty, who undoubtedly had faced years of incoming students as ill equipped as I was to take on the enormity of music's meaning. At once fearsome and terribly kind, our professors overlooked our laughable lack of knowledge and assured us that we would know all this, and maybe more, after four grueling years of study under the tutelage of their august minds.

A niche area of oddball ability earned me a reputation for being a savant. The dreaded exercise called "drop the needle"—too random to study for—allowed our professors to glean what our exposure to music had been thus far.

Records would be stacked on the phonograph, and the professor would literally drop the needle in the middle of the disk. We were given ten seconds to identify, first, the period of the music: Renaissance, baroque, classical, romantic, twentieth century, music of today. Then the composer: Gabrieli, Bach, Mozart, Beethoven, Brahms, Stravinsky, Carter. Then, if we were able to, the actual piece. Canzone, the *Goldberg* Variations, *Jupiter* Symphony, *Eroica* Symphony, *A German Requiem*, *Pulcinella* Suite, *Double Concerto*. And the last, infinitesimal, bonus detail: could we identify the orchestra or, if applicable, the performer as soloist? The point was to force us to keep listening and embrace areas of music that were yet unfamiliar.

"Tristan!"

I spat the word out on the first day of my music history class within two seconds after the needle dropped to the vinyl below. One massive cluster of a chord in two fleeting seconds: eureka! The famous half-diminished seventh chord that defined the opera *Tristan und Isolde* was the very sound that had crowded my ears from the good old days spent lying on my living-room carpet, listening through the din of a vacuum cleaner. Thanks, Mom.

"That's correct, Miss Butler. Very good."

Challenging as chess is for many, this game was tic-tac-toe for me. But I couldn't gloat. The certainty of my grotesque inadequacy in general far outweighed any confidence I might have gained from that game-show quiz. From my vantage point, all my classmates were brilliant and much more talented. And thrillingly familiar…I had found my tribe.

We students were a group of disparate people gathered together seemingly at random, because there was nothing else on this earth we could envision doing with our lives. That random congealing was the very element that felt dear, intimate, and true for us all. We didn't need to know each other, really—the rare and distinctive gene we had in common was a deep urge to parse out and understand the unknowable: music. We were somber and grave in the face of the task at hand. For many, including me, and surely for diverse reasons, this was a matter of death and then life.

Cramming my oboe and meager possessions into the maid's room off the kitchen of Mrs. S.'s twelve-room apartment, I prepared to settle in. Along with a single bed, a small chest of drawers, and a lamp, this former servant's patch of real estate from the beginning of the twentieth century provided not a full bath, not a half bath, but a "quarter bath." The bathtub was about twenty-four inches square in footprint. No showerhead, just a tub spout, and no sink in the room. It did have a toilet: a small blessing. Slapstick, with all four limbs sticking straight in the air, is the only way to describe my bathing experience, and it took me weeks to be able to orchestrate my daily ablutions with relative ease. Whichever way I chose to cleanse *any* part of myself, there was no such thing as a quick dip.

The now single Mrs. S. was on the prowl for a new man. Many suitors wined and dined her three evenings each and every week, the turnstile of her social life spinning potential stepfathers through the front door. She was a catch: a creamy, liquid blonde with a stunning apartment beautifully decorated in the traditional style.

Luxurious damask fabric covered the sumptuous down-stuffed sofas, and striped dupioni silks covered the club chairs. Pillows with perfect karate-chopped top edges were placed just so, with an expert designerlike eye. "Never enough pillows!" Mrs. S. would declare to the empty living room when she thought no one was listening. The curtains billowed down from ten-foot-high ceilings, layering sheers with swags, sandwiched between pinch-pleat side panels. The artwork was impressive: Klee, Miró, a Mondrian or two. Even *I* noticed that.

Mrs. S. insisted on 100 percent silk sheets, even for the kids, Whitney and David. Three mornings a week she slithered between those silk sheets, chatting on the phone while I looked after the children, getting them dressed and fed. How odd that she needed me to care for them while she was in the very next room, arranging luncheons with Mitzi and Buffy! When I was a young girl, my mother was also in close proximity yet not available—but I was blind to this irony. Mothers create separation from their children any way they find necessary and for whatever reason. Children cope, and this was all standard operating procedure for Whitney and David. They seemed happy enough.

Central Park was just down the block, and Mrs. S. absolutely insisted that the children go to "the Park" three mornings a week, rain or shine. That exclusive patch of grass was an Upper East

Side matter of privileged principle, after all. Hand in hand in hand, the children and I approached Fifth Avenue. Whitney was something of a rapscallion who had plans of her own. I knew it was coming but was never sure exactly when. At some point during the walk, Whitney would break from our pack. At times her method of disengaging from my hand was a kick or a bite, and she drew blood regularly. A trickster at heart, off she went into her blue yonder, leaving David and me first in the dust and then in pursuit.

That girl could run, and I had David in tow, so I had to think fast. He was a tiny boy, so I tucked him under my arm, positioned as a torpedo. As we ran after his sister, he stuck his arms straight out in front of him and willed his body go rigid. David had the instincts of an Apollo rocket.

Doormen on Fifth Avenue came to know us well, as the great chase replayed week after week.

Evenings were the only hours I could practice uninterrupted. On the nights I was in charge, I settled Whitney and David into their bedrooms, kissed them good night, walked to the other side of the huge apartment, and closed the door to my cubicle of a bedroom. After soaking my reeds and beginning my warm-up exercises, I soon began to hear little children by my door, mice scuttling in the dark. I ignored them.

My father bequeathed one gift to me as I left for college: his headphones. I threw them over my ears while the brats romped around the apartment, obviously trying to coax me out to play with them. But the dancing footsteps soon became loud bangs on my door, and their bedtime rituals were repeated over and over, eating up my precious practice time. If I was lucky, I began to practice in earnest at 10:00 p.m., and soon

Mrs. S. would be home and the night was a bust. She needed silence to sleep.

Because I took my child-care duties seriously, my practice routine never jelled. Whitney and David seemed to want me, but I did not want them. I was rough with them. At times I screamed and yanked their skinny arms to get their attention or to press my point, of course to no effect. As the weeks progressed I felt more and more anxious and on edge. I was missing out on my college life and neglecting my oboe, all because of these rotten kids.

It was odd and somewhat unnerving to live with a woman who was open with her emotions, not at all like my buttoned-up mother. Mrs. S. seemed like a trout out of water, flopping about and in need of air: she vacillated between hopefully cheerful and despairingly sad. And she was understandably morose at times, alluding to marital war stories with oblique asides. The husband was "In California." He was with "Another Woman." It was all "Very Difficult." What with "The Kids."

One night, Mrs. S. asked if I'd like to watch the movie *The Way We Were* on her video recorder. It had just been released in 1973, but she'd managed to get a bootleg copy from "The Coast." I loved Babs as much as the next red-blooded American, but this story was way beyond my life experience. What did I know about female Jewish political activism and redheaded goyim? I knew about doomed love, of course, from Tristan and Isolde, but I couldn't quite connect those dots to Barbra Streisand and Robert Redford.

At the conclusion of the movie and with a couple of martinis under her belt, Mrs. S. turned to me on the soft damask sofa, looking wistful.

"She just had too much love in her. She just loved him too damned much."

Her eyes brimmed with tears, and I felt I should say something to let her know that I understood, which I didn't.

"Did *you* love your husband too much?" I asked. That broke her momentary reverie.

"That bastard? He's dead to me."

She was off to her silk sheets; I to my hovel, quarter tub, and headphones.

Mrs. S.'s eyes grew large when I told her I would be moving out at the end of the semester.

"But why? The children adore you, and I really need your help, Marcia."

"They won't let me practice at night. You know how they won't go to bed. I'm really sorry, but I need to practice twice as much, and I can't because the kids are not behaving well."

"But they're so attached to you. Can't you see it?"

"Not really... I wasn't aware..."

I saw myself as the evil babysitter, a real Marquis de Sade, silently gleeful, with a full-on case of schadenfreude when they scraped their knees or scratched each other while fighting. Apparently, those children saw me differently—as a new member of the family—and I was rendered speechless by Mrs. S. as she urged me to reconsider.

Tears began to slide down my cheeks as she explained how they needed me and enjoyed my company around the apartment. I was wanted, maybe even loved. But I couldn't do it, and I had a terrible sense of rejecting something—family—I spent my life longing for. I bawled for a few minutes while she stood with her delicate arms around me, our bodies not touching—the doyenne way.

"Well, I see that you're upset, and I guess we'll just find someone else."

"I'm sorry. Thank you."

I went into my cubicle and crawled in between the silk sheets that Mrs. S. insisted I, too, sleep on. My eyes scanned the small bedroom, once nude of possessions, now jammed with all the stuff of a starting life, according to Mrs. S. Special soaps, lotions, and toiletries I never dreamed existed, much less knew were necessary, that appeared in my room when she made a trip to the high-end apothecary. A radio she'd purchased for me because she wanted me to tune in to the classical music station she thought I'd enjoy. A dress lying at the foot of my bed she'd surprised me with for my very first student recital at Mannes. My very own dress. The stack of programs she'd always left in my room from the Metropolitan Opera productions and the New York Philharmonic concerts she'd attended with her dates, so I could study the program notes. The empty plastic wrappers of the pocket-size Kleenex packets she'd jam into my purse each and every time I left with the kids to go to Central Park, so I could wipe their snotty noses. And some of those plastic dead soldiers were from the packets of tissues she'd quietly left outside my closed door when she heard me crying in my room (she never asked why, and I loved her for that), because Mrs. S. didn't want me to use common toilet paper to wipe my own snotty nose. A full LP set of the entire opera of *Tristan und Isolde* that just appeared in my room one day. It was from her personal collection. The Flagstad version.

I slipped the last side of *Tristan* out of its jacket and plopped it onto my small record player, also courtesy of Mrs. S., clamped my father's headphones around my ears, and dropped the needle onto the grooves. As I turned up the volume, the "Liebestod" throbbed into my head. I lay back on the bed and sobbed for everything I didn't understand and violently willed myself to revert back to my life alone with my oboe. During the last minute of the "Liebestod," as Wagner finally allows the harmony to resolve, I sat up, rigid, and understood something: I was a terrible and hollow girl.

Just a week or so later, at Christmas break, I left Mrs. S. and the brats. I saw her once more on the street in front of Mannes several months later. She had accepted a proposal of marriage from one of her suitors. The apartment was up for sale, as they were to move to Boston soon.

See? I thought to myself on hearing this. She would have left in any case.

Impressive

Entering music conservatory on a full scholarship, you think you're pretty damned good. The school asks you to take part in the first student recital of the semester. Held once a week, these are noontime performances during which students play pieces they've worked up to a fairly high level. Accepting the invitation, of course, you decide to play the first movement of the Hindemith Oboe Sonata.

A few days later, you have your very first oboe lesson. You don't know this man and are eager to impress him with your playing, just the way you seem to have impressed everyone else. As you play the Hindemith Oboe Sonata, to be performed in just one week, he guides you through the movement and gives some suggestions. Then at the end of the lesson he says that you can go ahead and perform the Hindemith, but at the next lesson he will be asking you to play nothing but long tones. And he suspects that you'll need to do this for months, possibly till the end of the semester.

You crumble.

Long tones mean that you play one note for as long as you can hold it. And then you play the next note for as long as possible, and on and on. He explains that you are going to have to go back to the basics, because he hears problems in your playing. You're not quite as solid as you should be. Three months. Maybe longer, depending on your progress. You accept this news silently. Then you go back to your room across the street at Mrs. S.'s apartment and sob for the next four hours nonstop. Thank goodness it's an off night for the kids. You wake up the next morning and set to crying some more. You cry on and off throughout the entire week and finally pull yourself together enough to perform the Hindemith Oboe Sonata. Everyone seems to be impressed.

You walk into the next lesson and play the long tones for a solid hour with your new teacher. After listening and making comments and suggestions, he tells you to go home and practice nothing but long tones for at least three hours each day. No music at all. You go back to the apartment and cry a bunch more. But damn it, you play long tones for three hours. No music. That is hard to do.

At the next lesson, he tells you to do the exact same thing for the following week's lesson. The days move along slowly, and you don't feel nearly as impressive as you did two weeks ago, before this whole long-tone thing cropped up. You've stopped crying by now, because it's just a waste of time. The time spent crying could be used for playing the long tones. You do as you're told.

At the third long-tone lesson (after playing a bunch of long tones for him), he stares at you for about fifteen endless seconds. You think he's going to lambaste you for sounding like shit. Instead he says that you don't have to play long tones anymore. He says that you have made the most rapid and complete progress of any student he has ever taught. He says he is impressed. You go home and cry for a few minutes. Then you start to play music.

Thief

My final tagline—"I have to get away from those kids"—was surely what resonated with her. My mother wholeheartedly concurred. Why hadn't I started with that simple declaration?

Instead I began with a typically well-thought-out formal proposal, as if for a doctoral thesis: "How I Might Die If I Do Not Leave the Free Digs of Mrs. S." Written and rewritten, stated with irrefutable and lockstep logic as to why I needed to be released from my sweet deal with Mrs. S. Reasons: strong and weak. Alternative options: with footnotes as backup. Reverse psychology: Freud versus Jung. These necessary and well-documented lists, all committed to both paper and memory, preceded the nail-biting call to my mother, when I would present my orals, defend my position, and implore her for money to pay my rent.

Always begin with the postulate: what you assume to be true and what you then hope to prove. It's the heart of the scientific method, after all. My mother didn't like children very much, and I'd forgotten all about that, even just four months out of the Butler household. I should have gone right to that mother lode—that we both hated kids—as I contemplated what I thought would be the most difficult problem to surmount: her worries about money.

But she'd pay. Fifty dollars a month was to be my allowance toward the rent for staying in the apartment of a wealthy Korean American piano student who lived across town from Mannes on the Upper West Side. She had taken pity on me after witnessing several excruciating episodes with Whitney in front of the school. It was a mercy deal, pure and simple. She didn't particularly need my money. But I gratefully paid and took up residency in a corner of her living room, sleeping on the small sofa.

I had clothing. Now I had shelter. But I still needed food. My mother never asked how I was going to negotiate this third necessity of life and just assumed I would make it all work. I had some cash saved from money given to me by my grandparents, which held me for a few weeks until I figured things out.

I was determined. I was methodical. I was hungry. So I became a thief.

A fellow oboe student was producing blank metal slugs as a substitute for subway tokens and doled them out to all the Mannes students who didn't see it as a crime to rob the New York City subway system of a fare. I gladly filled my pockets with the phony tokens: a savings of thirty-five cents per ride, the cost of subway fare in 1974. After several months, cops began to appear daily at the East 77th Street station. Policemen scrutinized the hands of passengers going through the turnstiles, and we had to be wily to slip past them. Many students gave it up for fear of getting arrested; a few unlucky pianists had been nabbed and booked. But I continued to take my chances.

A life of hunger necessitated further deviousness. I took a three-pronged approach, with my roommate as my dupe.

She was careless. Coins slipped out of her pockets, finding their way down the sides of the cushions of her sofa and club chairs. I searched the furniture crevices daily for loose change.

Her kitchen was overstocked. I couldn't just open her refrigerator and help myself, as I had with Mrs. S.'s newfangled Sub-Zero. But very carefully and incrementally, I began to siphon off food from her: just the right amount, so she wouldn't notice.

And only when absolutely necessary, I took a few single dollar bills from her wallet while she slept in the bedroom. I rationalized that taking the food and coins was not really stealing. After all, she would never look for pennies and dimes in her own furniture. And she would probably never notice the missing food. Perhaps. Taking the dollar bills? *That* was stealing. The guilt felt like another entity living in my belly, although it was easier to ignore than the hunger pangs.

Fortunately my roommate and I shared a rigorous discipline for practicing, so we didn't have much time for lounging around and getting to know each other. I avoided her eyes, because surely if we looked directly at each other, she would immediately finger the thief she'd let into her home.

But my stomach still ached. As I tried to sleep lying on my back, with my legs draped over the arms of the sofa, the concave curve of my belly reached all the way to my spine. I pressed down hard with my fists, trying to confuse the hunger pangs that woke me throughout the night. I was hanging on, one saltine at a time.

A brilliant solution emerged: Steve Adelstein, my oboe teacher and the man of the long tones. He was a quirky pedagogue—mildly misanthropic, failing at love affairs, obsessing over reed making, suffering from compulsive disorders, ballooning from overeating. How rare this man was for a young girl who grew up in a family where absolutely everything was hidden, undisclosed, and unspoken. Adelstein opened his veins and bled out, telling all his gory, unedited truths.

How I loved Adelstein; and that is how all his students and I referred to him. He smelled of sweet vulnerability, yet there was not one whiff of male-female dynamic between us. We were more like neutered buddies, and he maintained the dynamic impeccably. Kindred spirits, we both presented to the world as teetering on weird. In fact, privately, I called him Adelweird.

After the oboe, food was the subject on the tip of Adelweird's tongue. He'd been obese on and off throughout his life and struggled mightily with his addiction. But he'd found a way to keep his weight in check. For lunch, he enjoyed a robust head of iceberg lettuce, cut into quarters with a low-calorie salad dressing and a diet cola. This "meal," served at the Blue Skyline Diner, around the corner from Mannes, was enough to keep him going throughout his day of teaching. It filled him up, kept the hunger pangs away, yet had very few calories, which he counted assiduously.

Eureka! I didn't give a damn about those calories. While Adelweird was steadfastly trying to lose weight, I was desperately trying to fill up. My *only* meal of the day became an entire head of iceberg lettuce with the stem cut off. Unshredded. Unripped. Pure and unadulterated. With Russian dressing. On the side. I imagined that the bits of pickle floating within the dressing were of added nutritional value.

"Yes, miss, what would you like today?"

"I'll have a head of iceberg lettuce, please."

"Dressing? We have Italian, Russian, blue cheese, and oil and vinegar."

"Russian, please."

"The whole bottle? Again?"

"Yes, please."

"HEADOFICEBERGLETTUCEBOTTLERUSSIANDRES
SINGONSIDE—PEEEK UP!!!!"

The waiters and I reenacted our formalized Greek diner performance every day. Shepherding me to the rear of the restaurant, where I sheepishly sat with my back to the door, my waiter
presented the head to me on a large plate. Turning it upside
down, I carefully fanned the leaves out to make space for the
Russian dressing to dribble down into its deep crevices. The ritual was exacting: just a bit of dressing at a time, so that the head
could be completely saturated with the "nourishing" creaminess
that would keep me sated until bedtime. This took about a half
bottle per meal.

On occasion, when they felt generous, the waiters brought a
few slices of Wonder Bread, and I smeared on as much oleo as
possible. This starch and lard were a perfect complement to my
vitamin- and carb-deficient roughage. And, rarely, my favorite
Greek waiter took pity on me and laid a few strips of processed
turkey on top of the head, like a few strands of hair on a bald-
ing pate. He offered bacon only one time, which I righteously
eschewed. I was a thief, but I had my principles: I now practically
fancied myself a vegetarian.

By bedtime, my belly was still stuffed with a partially digested
stew of Russian dressing, iceberg lettuce, Wonder Bread, and
oleo. I slept like a baby, dreaming of pale green heads bobbing
over the rough waters of my gurgling tummy.

Hell

First you contact a guy in the South of France who has a bamboo farm through which you purchase some stalks. They come in the mail in big boxes, and you store them, praying that the quality is good, very good. But there are no guarantees. It could be crap. You soak these stalks, called tube cane, in water for an hour or so to soften them up.

You select one stalk, which is about eight inches long and a half inch in diameter. You use a razor blade to slice the tube lengthwise in three equal parts. You now have three slender stalks.

You have a thing called a gouging machine, a precision piece of machinery that will gouge out the thickness of the dissected tube from the inside, at the pithy part, so that it is very thin, about two millimeters.

You cut the gouged piece short, about four and a half inches in length.

You continue to soak the newly gouged cut cane. Then you crease this piece at the center point with a very sharp reed knife and fold it over, horizontally, in half.

You place this folded piece of cane onto a thing called a

shaper tip, another precision device that allows you to shave down the sides of the cane with a razor blade at an exact contour, which makes every piece consistent.

You have these things called tubes, which are tapered brass tubes about forty-six millimeters in length with cork wrapped around one end. That's the end that will be inserted into the top of the oboe. The other end, which is the smaller opening, is where you place the folded cane.

You tie a strand of nylon from a spool of thread onto a spoke on the back of a chair. This anchoring point allows you to neatly wind and wrap the folded cane onto this metal tube with the thread. You have now produced what is called a blank.

Now comes the hard part, the artistry. You have to have a reed knife that is razor sharp. You spend a lot of time sharpening the knife on a whetstone. You carve this blank down so that the two sides, when scraped enough, just perfectly, will vibrate when air is blown into them. The top, at the opening, is feather thin and has been clipped open. This reed is what is inserted into the top of the oboe and will make the sound when you blow into it.

You've scraped and scraped and tested the reed and played on it a bit. You adjust it and rescrape and clip it more and play on it. Then you decide that the cane is bad, too soft or too hard. Or you didn't scrape it perfectly, or it just doesn't sound the way you want. You let it dry out and pick it up the next day, hoping that it will have settled a bit, and you rework it and rescrape it.

Then you throw it out and start over.

A Job

AFTER FOUR MONTHS of passing lettuce through my guts, I realized if I was going to stay alive through the next three years of music conservatory training, I needed to get serious about supporting myself.

A gruff but kind Greek restaurant owner showed some mercy and hired me, with no experience, as a waitress four evenings a week at his Greenwich Village "English pub–style" restaurant. I was assured a meal before work, and that alone seemed sufficient pay. Dining at the beginning of each shift, I also managed to stuff more food down my gullet at the end of the night. Nick the Greek didn't seem to resent my double-dipping on the food. It was obvious I had a lot of catching up to do. And the tips were good.

My best buddy and fellow opera devotee extraordinaire was a bar patron named Rupert, a middle-aged Austrian businessman working in New York City. In addition to a mutual love of opera, we had that more rarefied opera gene in common: we were both Wagner freaks.

Rupert was a jovial eccentric. Wagner aside, he could have played a perfect caricature side role in an opera buffa by Rossini. And he was rich, or so it seemed to me, as he pulled wads of hundred-dollar bills out of his solid-gold money clip. I marveled at his invariably impeccable appearance: silk shirt, woolen sweater vest, suit jacket, and a red pocket square in the left breast pocket. His hair remained perfectly coiffed with oil, well before styling gel hit the cosmetics shelves. The only items missing to complete his costume were a watch fob and pince-nez! Yet even with all this careful layering and a heavy-handed aftershave, he exuded a slightly sickening odor that could not be encapsulated beneath his layered clothing—something unhealthy. Maybe it was just a new European odor, unfamiliar to me.

Gin martinis were Rupert's customary early evening drinks, and as the evening wore on and his cravat loosened, he graduated to sweet Riesling wine, all served up by Tony, the redheaded Irish bartender. In the time between serving my customers their $12.95 prix fixe roast beef dinners and Rupert's three-martini limit, we talked about Wagner and Kirsten and whoever else were the singers of the day with passionate, opinionated vehemence. He certainly had his convictions, and I'm sure that he could not have been more surprised to meet a mere waitress who had her *own* views and knew as much as he did on the subject of our mutually beloved Wagner.

"Marcia, which recording of *Tristan* do you prefer? The live 1952 Furtwängler version vit Flagstad or the 1966 set vit Nilsson conducted by Karl Böhm?"

He frequently baited this trap, his eyes sly with the setup. We were easy with each other, and Rupert loved to goad me because he knew my devotion to Kirsten could not be shaken.

"Please, Rupert. I'm not going to grace that question with an answer. But just for the record, I will *repeat:* Isolde has never had a finer portrayer than Kirsten Flagstad. Period, end of opera."

"Ya, ya, that's vat I thought you'd say. I vas just making sure."

His eyes betrayed amusement at my expense. But this subject was not a laughing matter.

"Well, I'm saying it *again* because it's true."

The bell rang three times from the kitchen: a signal that food was ready. Spinning on my heel, I dramatically sashayed through the dining room and into the kitchen to pick up the order.

Nick appeared completely baffled by his bar patron Rupert—who dropped a tidy wad of money on booze several evenings a week—and his friendship with this inexperienced waitress. When Rupert and I inevitably began to caress the tender subject of my beloved Kirsten Flagstad yet *again,* Nick, clearly out of his league, would shrug and walk back to the kitchen to scream at the line cooks.

Rupert had met his match, and most evenings we were happily "off to the opera," discussing the various shadings of a tenor's high C and a soprano's high A.

"Ya, Ya, Birgit. She really ees surpassing Kirsten now. I heard her in Vienna last year. That voice! That presence! Ya. Ya."

Rupert's thick Austrian accent became slow and exaggerated as he downed his third martini. He was at it again and had to be corrected.

"No, Rupert! No, no, no! How can you be disloyal to Kirsten? No one even comes close!"

"Ya. Ya. Vell, vait until Birgit comes to the Met next season for da *Ring* cycle und you vill hear vat I mean. Ya. Ya."

I kept my mouth shut on that one. I could never afford even one ticket to the Metropolitan Opera, let alone the entire four operas in the *Ring* cycle.

During the 1930s, '40s, and '50s, Kirsten had been the

pinnacle soprano of Wagner heroine roles. Swedish singer Birgit
Nilsson was the reigning queen in the '70s, and Rupert had fallen
head over heels *daffy* for Birgit. Talk about a head voice! As the
evenings wore on, Rupert loved to recount to anyone who'd listen the famous story of Nilsson during an outdoor performance
of *Turandot* in Italy. When she rendered one high C, the citizens
of the town thought the fire alarm had sounded.

That little hole-in-the-wall restaurant held a group of people
utterly unlike my family or my fellow music students. Now in
my second year of school, I played the role of music-student
waitress who chatted with Rupert. I could control how much I
revealed of my life, surely the main draw for anyone who fre-
quents watering holes. A bar is particularly appealing because it
mimics a sense of bubbled privacy and also presents the freedom
to take risks, if only for a few hours. You could always walk out at
the end of the shift, to be who you were or even whomever you
wanted to be.

The truth was I'd become a promiscuous young woman during
my first year at Mannes—exclusively one-night stands, sometimes with students at Mannes who wondered why I never gave
them eye contact again, and sometimes with pickups in the "lettuce" corner coffee shop. I was dipping my toes into brackish waters. My father had set the template.

With Rupert the Austrian, Nick the Greek, and Irish Tony
as my witnesses, this job became the stage where I began an
unconscious search for a new Wotan. The imprint of my father, of what men wanted from me, was deeply tattooed onto
my fragile skin. I'd pick that scab and let it bleed, because now
I had the privacy to play it out. While I lived alone in a studio
apartment I could just afford in the then-undeveloped neigh-

borhood of Chelsea, my father would resurrect before me, now as a reconstructed opera villain with whom I would negotiate ancient yet familiar terms: unquestioning and always silent. I believed they were *my* desires; I did not own what my father gave me.

Glass

HE WALKED INTO the bar one night, a very tall—maybe six feet four—prematurely graying man dressed in jeans and a jean shirt. I noticed pockmarks on his stubbly cheeks, a full mustache, and a hooded look in his eyes. He may have been drunk; I couldn't tell as he walked slowly, gracefully, almost, and glided onto a bar stool. He nodded to Tony.

"Ouzo, beer back." Zipping that down his throat in a single swallow, he pushed the shot glass toward Tony.

"Another, please."

"Sure, Steve. We haven't seen you in a while. How are things?"

"Busy. Very busy."

Throughout that evening, as I wandered back and forth from the service bar to the dining room, I was aware of this man. The potent shots of ouzo didn't appear to faze him. Tony kept shoving more ouzo toward him, topping off the beer as needed. Other bar patrons, including Rupert, seemed to keep their distance, giving him a wide drinking berth. He was a big man with a dangerous aura. I kept my intrigued, reckless eyes on him.

Just before closing time, as I was cashing in my singles and change in tips for bigger bills, I heard a commotion at the end of the bar where Ouzo Steve, as people were calling him, was seated. He had gathered a few late-night drinkers as an audience. Everyone cheered and clapped at what Steve had just demonstrated. I looked up, curious.

"What happened?"

"Ya. Ya. He just ate a vineglass! Ya, ya, Marcia, come quick to see dis thing vat he did."

If Rupert was impressed, I wanted to see. I trotted over from the service bar and saw the stem of a broken wineglass lying on the bar.

"Do it again," I said, not knowing what, exactly, had been done.

Steve obliged. Carefully placing a fresh and intact wineglass to his lips, he gathered his teeth on the top and bottom of the rim and in a swift motion snapped the glass downward. The broken pieces remained inside his mouth. He began to chew. I could hear the disturbing crunch of the glass shards against his back molars. He chewed carefully for at least sixty seconds. The bar was silent, rapt. Then in one big, dramatic gulp, he swallowed the pulverized glass.

"Do it again."

Steve looked at me and nodded. Another glass bit the dust.

"Do it *again*."

A sly smile crept across Steve's mouth. He aimed to please me. The bar crowd quickly dissipated, and Tony turned his back to busy himself, wiping wineglasses.

Three times he'd had his fill. I was charmed.

It was well past midnight, and everyone was preparing to leave, patrons and employees alike. Nick wanted to lock up.

Steve nodded my way. He had steel-blue eyes: real beauties, like marbles. With an imperceptible nod of my head, we silently agreed. As I reached for my purse and coat, Tony stepped out from behind the bar to block my exit. He pressed his face close to mine, his hands on either cheek.

"I *saw* that. Marcia, *no*. Not this one. Think about this. *Please.*"

Tony knew me. He was playing Rigoletto, protecting his virginal daughter, Gilda. But I was no virgin. I was leading a double sort of life: disciplined second-year music student at the Mannes College of Music by day, one-night-stand girl by night. Rupert was not interested in me in that way. We loved each other from across a Wagnerian stage. I'd tried Tony only once. He was much too nice: I sensed his need to protect me, and I would gently rebuff him after that one night together. Newly emboldened by the privacy my studio apartment afforded me, I was drawn only to dubious, unknowable, and possibly dangerous men. Tony, Nick, Rupert, and surely others had witnessed my sly, slithering exits at the end of my shifts. I called my conquests my yes men.

Tony's green Irish eyes were now boring into mine, trying to get my attention and slapping me awake. I said nothing, dragging my eyes away from his face, trying to look at the floor. He grabbed my face more roughly and pinched my cheek flesh hard.

"Ouch!"

Rupert's head snapped in our direction, and he quickly grabbed his coat and left. Nick had shepherded out all the patrons, leaving just the staff. I could see Steve waiting outside for me, smoking.

"Marcia. Wake the fook up. This is yer life here. I said *no*."

"Why not? And who the hell are *you*, anyway?"

"I'm yer guardian angel tonight. You can't figure this one out?

The man carries a gun around, fer fook's sake. Jaysus, Mary, and Joseph and all the *fooking* holy martyrs."

Hearing it clearly, I took two quick breaths.

"I'm *fine*. Now kindly fuck off."

Tony's fingers entwined with mine, and he pulled sharply down on my hands to get my body closer to his, for an emphasis I would not acknowledge.

"*Jaysus,* Marcia. You just don't know. I'm *warning* you. Not. This. One."

"Christ, Tony. Just let *go* of me!"

Startled, he pulled his hands away quickly and stepped back, as if realizing for the first time that he didn't really know me at all. We'd finished spitting our whispered screams at each other. I pushed past Tony out the door and into a cab with Steve. After years on my father's lap, my male object of desire was pure and simple: I had to fear him; I needed the danger. And I said yes to it all. Steve was my man, at least for that night, and who knew what would come of it? Tony's protective warning simply inspired me. New stage. New opera.

Elliott

As an oboist specializing in contemporary music, you accept prestigious invitations from living composers—but the next one humbles you. You're asked to play in a celebratory birthday concert for Elliott Carter, but further, you'll be the first American to perform his oboe concerto. This work, written for the venerable Swiss oboist Heinz Holliger in 1986, is considered one of the most difficult pieces ever written for the oboe. The prospect is invigorating but also daunting. After two days of thought, you take a deep breath and agree.

Upon receiving the score, you can't play the piece or even do a cursory read-through. This is an understatement. You can't play a single bar at tempo or, in most cases, even three consecutive notes. You have to figure out how to cut into this massive behemoth. First, learn the notes. Forget about making music at this point. Just learn the damned notes. Your practice sessions consist of setting the metronome at an unspeakably slow tempo and then playing one bar over and over until you can go one notch faster. You make sure that you can play the bar correctly before you increase the speed. Many times, pushing that notch up can take several days. You have six months to prepare the piece, but after three months, you're in a full-out panic. You're not even halfway through where you think you need to be in order to perform the work.

As this reality sets in, you consider backing out. Certainly there is not sufficient time for another oboist to prepare. Not many oboists in the world would accept an invitation to perform this piece in the first place, because this is in such a specialty niche of difficulty. You anticipate the humiliation that would overcome you if you give up. You would have to admit to yourself that you're just not good enough; you don't have the talent or the goods. You're mediocre... average. You see yourself as a contemporary music specialist, yet in reality maybe you are just a fraud.

The grinding rub chafes at you day after day. There are of course many moments when you are able to nudge that metronome up one notch, and you allow yourself to be secretly gleeful. Oh, goody! Some progress. But you try not to get too happy because there are so many more notches to go. Thousands upon thousands of notches. It all feels so endless. Yet you are aware on a very subtle level that the work is finding its way into your bones and muscles and blood and guts.

You remember the exact passage when the cogs lock together. It is not even the hardest section, technically, but what you begin to hear is music. There's music in there, and it is actually you making that music. Your stomach rolls over, a love swoon. The physical sensation is visceral and distinct. It is a very private knowing; a merging with something divine, precious, and rare. As a musician, you covet those moments. You live and play for them. It is a truly deep connection with the composer, as if you channel his inner life. A tender synergy is present, and you fear *that to even speak about it will dissipate it immediately. Don't talk. Just be aware.*

From that moment on, things start to roll. You continue to plod away, but the carrot—Elliott Carter's music—is now in plain sight, right in front of you. You still must conquer technical aspects, but that technique is now truly in service to the voice of a composer. The hierarchy has reversed, and the process is properly aligned. The music eventually shows you the way and becomes the solution. You feel like you've come back from the dead.

You're ready to start rehearsals with the orchestra. You've already played the thing through for Carter, and he seems to be impressed. His wife has taken a liking to you for some reason and sends you postcards from their house in Connecticut, writing stuff like "I hope life is treating you well." She must know, somehow, that the only thing you are doing these days is practicing and making reeds for her husband's concerto.

The day of the concert, your life is about to crack wide open. Elliott Carter ambles onstage and accepts the good wishes from the audience for his eighty-fifth birthday. (He will live to the age of 103, composing all the way.) You're standing backstage, pacing around. You want the concert to be pure and perfect and reflect all your unimaginably hard work. How will anyone really know what you've done?

The audience starts to clap. You have been announced. You walk out onstage and put the oboe in your mouth. You take that breath, and for the next twenty minutes you concentrate with such ferocity that the audience before you disappears. It's you, the oboe, the orchestra, and the music. The clapping begins again.

Don G.

DON GIOVANNI: THE devil's earthly alter ego. He's the man you should hate because he breaks society's rules and never apologizes or even explains. Steve. My Don G.

Meeting when I got off work, we would go on "dates" that generally consisted of barhopping. I didn't even drink much, but Don G. proved to be a falling-down drunk. This regular incapacitation was a welcome relief I came to count on: at the end of the evening I could always throw him in a cab, without an argument, without negotiation. This made me feel immensely powerful, an illusion that I actually controlled him.

He was ignorant about music but did know a lot about the New York City art world, knowledge that he slipped into conversation from time to time. Steve was a decade older, and I was appropriately impressed with his worldly aura, but that wasn't what pulled me to him. He could have been the best of friends with Leo Castelli for all I cared. No, I was enamored of his undisciplined manner and his unfiltered Camel cigarettes, including the loose flecks of tobacco he was always spitting off his tongue. The bedroom slippers he'd wear on the street instead of proper shoes. And the glass he continued to chew. I never got enough of those hidden masticated shards.

So many infinitesimally enormous details didn't quite add up. He carried a gun. I didn't know if it was loaded and never asked. I willed myself to go blank on the disturbing parts, like the many creepy men he'd nod to while we were out and about. Who are they, I'd ask occasionally. He remained silent with not even so much as a placating noise. I never got an answer, and it didn't seem to matter. I was in love and blind and blank and agreeable.

We had careless sex when he could stand up—or lie down, as the case might require. He would toss the gun next to my oboe on my reed desk, and we'd set to the act in a hasty and perfunctory manner; very soon I found myself pregnant. Now the oboe-playing waitress had really faltered.

Having such a cordoned-off life made sharing news of the pregnancy with anyone virtually impossible. Mannes, music, the oboe, the bar, Steve. My father. They were all strictly separate categories where the lines of demarcation had to remain sharply drawn. And secret. This compartmentalization was both conscious and unconscious and had served me well from the minute I was born, it seemed.

Now I would risk mingling my categories. For the first time in my young life, I thought I might not be able to handle things on my own. I was in trouble. Impulsively, I thought of my mother, hoping that *this* might be the event that would interest her in me. The call was made.

"Mom? Mom, I'm really, *really* sorry. I'm pregnant."

The who, the what, and the why were trifling trivia. With uncomfortable run-on sentences, I quickly reassured my mother that all was well in New York City.

"But I already called my gynecologist and I'm taking care of it....In about two and a half more months...because he says that the fetus has to be formed more completely for the vacuum cleaner to work well.... The *vacuum cleaner.* That's the thing that they use to suction it out. It's like the Hoover, Mom.... Well, that's what he *said* to do, so I'll just wait, I guess. Yes, I can still work and go to school and practice. And everything..."

My mother was a master at small talk. Somehow she was able to eliminate silence whenever that dead air space might evoke disclosure or lead to understanding and, eventually, closeness. I was used to this tactic by now, and I snapped to like a good little soldier. I knew to talk fast and get all the information out quickly. And she had little to say because I had things well in hand. Of course they weren't, but within the first few seconds of the call, I'd realized my mistake. My mother, placated with a two-minute phone call, was satisfied with her efficient daughter's ability to resolve an easily righted gaffe, especially now that I'd been able to summon up the specter of the family Hoover.

It wasn't easy to play the oboe while hiding a pregnancy, with a belly that now formed a convex shape rather than the starved concave hollow from the previous Year of Lettuce. The three months I waited for the scheduled procedure dragged on to a miserable funeral cadence. Day after day, nausea roiled up at the most inconvenient times: in orchestra rehearsal, in classes, at work, and even on the subway. My days were spent doing just what I needed to do and no more. As Steve backed off, I remained happiest alone in bed, dead asleep, my only real respite from the scathing shame of my mistake and all my other secrets.

Yet reality pressed and pressed upon me, because I had managed to win the concerto competition at the Mannes College of Music. I could not avoid being a public spectacle.

97

"Congratulations, Marcia! You worked so hard, and it really paid off. The committee was unanimous."

Steve Adelweird was very proud of his most diligent of students. If he knew the truth about me, I would surely lose my best Mannes buddy in misanthropy. Feeling unworthy in so many ways, I remained silent, unable to accept his compliment. Adelweird looked at me and paused. Then, accepting my mood, he got right down to business, thankfully.

"Okay. Let's hear some long tones and scales."

I warmed up on a few notes to see if my reed was working. After a few good old long tones, Adelweird stopped me.

"Marcia, do you hear that oscillating? Why aren't you able to keep the sound steady? Try it again."

We spent most of the hour-long lesson trying to get my diaphragm to settle down and stop stuttering, just as we did in the very first lessons at the beginning of my studies. I had regressed before his eyes, and he was frustrated. I looked at the clock. Only seven more minutes of the lesson, and I was sounding like a rank beginner. This from the oboist who just won a big conservatory competition. Adelweird stopped me and stared.

"What the hell is wrong? This isn't your style."

"Nothing."

"Come on."

"Nothing!"

"I don't believe you."

"I'm just tired.... And I haven't been eating well. My stomach's upset."

"The restaurant's feeding you, right? I see you've gained a bit of weight, which is good."

"Yeah, they're feeding me. I'm just having trouble with other classes. I've had absences. I'm just really tired and…sleeping a lot."

I tried throwing him the right lines. Couldn't he figure it out? But no, as much as I toyed with teasing it out for him, I couldn't let this cat out of the bag.

"But I'm fine. Really. Let's just finish."

"Marcia, that's bullshit. You can't hold a straight tone! We're not leaving this room until you tell me. I know when you're not right."

Not right. How to explain in the four remaining minutes of my lesson all about the awful girl standing in front of him with an oboe in her hand?

In what felt like slow motion, I pulled my reed out of the oboe, returned it carefully to its small box, and placed the instrument down on the piano—a no-no in this school. Nothing was to be laid on top of pianos. Adelweird backed away from me, understanding the oddness of my behavior, as I walked to the corner of the room and leaned into the right angle. Laying my head heavily against it, I slid down into a crouching position on my haunches, my back to the room. The tears came. I could not look at him as I wailed. Unearthly moans came and came. No wonder the oboe's sound shook. A roiling hell was in my belly and had been waiting for this exact moment, when it could release its immense, searing pressure.

Adelweird went to the door of the studio and locked it. *Click.* I heard him walk back to me. He stood right at my back and did nothing. He was not my father, standing over Jinx in the corner of a stairway landing after delivering a knockout punch. The heat of his body was warm and alive and compassionate. Motionless, he was witnessing his brilliant student fall into a billion shards of glass. The oscillating of my shaky diaphragm was the very final outward expression of a wound so deep and so ancient I would never see the first slice. It would never heal, and if it did, the scar would go on forever.

I never told Adelweird. He never asked again. I didn't know what real love felt like, but that afternoon I imagined I had gently brushed up against a benign and safe love.

After three months of intense fatigue and morning sickness, the deed was done in an office with just a Valium to relax me. I was wide awake and afraid. And alone. A kind, well-meaning nurse sat by my head during the procedure and gripped my hand tightly, repeating, "Almost done. Almost done." For twenty unbearably long minutes I squeezed back, surely hurting her hand, trying to deflect the horrendous pain I was unprepared for. When the din stopped, I sat up and coldly scrutinized the special Hoover the doctor had used.

Those were the days when you could get an abortion without anesthesia, making it possible to walk straight out of the office onto the streets of New York City alone to stroll down Fifth Avenue. You might turn into a bright and alive Central Park and wander over to Tavern on the Green. A club sandwich with french fries would nicely satisfy your appetite, which had miraculously returned. And finally, you could go home to your apartment and feel such a blissfully welcome surge of energy you would pull your *own* Hoover out of the closet and clean the hell out of your dirty carpet. Even on a weekday.

As I vacuumed, I waited. Waited for the call. Waited for my mother to actually be a mother to her just barely twenty-year-old younger daughter. Waited and remembered that I had pretended that the face of the nurse I gazed at throughout the twenty-minute abortion was the face of my mother.

Kirsten sang:

Do I alone hear this melody...

Texas

Four hundred miles. That is the typical daily distance you drive while you're on tour with a woodwind quintet. Up at 6:00 a.m., into the car by 7:00 a.m., then driving all day while noshing on the remnants of the food from the reception the night before. (It's written in your contract that you get to take all the food provided at the concert reception if you want to.) You drive for eight hours, check into the motel, then go directly to the hall for a sound check; you eat a quick dinner, play the concert, go to the reception and meet the audience, get back to the motel at 11:30 p.m.

This is a glorious grind; a work schedule you treasure and look forward to, because it is rare to have the opportunity to perform the same program over and over—night after night. The first performance is vastly different from the twentieth. That difference is you and how you've come to explore and further understand music through repetition. Music, a malleable wonder, needs this evolution.

Now you're in Texas, and life on the road, although mostly tedious, can get interesting. Before drifting off to sleep, you notice that your room phone doesn't work—no worries; you'll call into your machine at the gas station the next day. John, the French horn player, is in the adjacent room, and he knocks on your wall: a little rhythm you've gotten into during the tour — just a good-night tap. But you're in Texas this particular night, and they like to party there in motel rooms.

"Kill me; please kill me!" You wake up with a start to hear two guys, drunk, raging, directly outside your door. One person wants to die; the other must be considering granting his wish. Over and over: "Kill me; please kill me." They weigh the pros and the cons, the whys and the why nots. Who will miss him? Who won't? Why he's worthless but who needs him to stay alive — a wife and baby son. His mother. His father is a "son of a bitch motherfucker," apparently.

Afraid to move a muscle, you're sleepless and have no choice but to eavesdrop. Ghoulishly drawn in, you're mostly scared shitless, because you don't want to die this particular night from a spray of rogue buckshot. Such anguish is difficult to witness, even siphoned through the goopy gauze of booze or drugs and the thin door of a cheap motel room. For two long hours.

John taps on the wall. He's most likely tried calling your room, but to no avail. You tap back, then jam cotton into your ears. Six a.m. comes suddenly, the sun roaring through the stained curtains. You open the door and stick your head out. John walks up, carrying coffee for you. He shrugs — no blood. Seven a.m., bags tucked in the car. Nestled in the backseat, you position your headphones and dial up your Mozart, girding yourself for the eight-hour ride ahead as you munch on room-temperature cold cuts for breakfast. And you wonder how Texas will alter the music at the concert tonight.

In C

Five o'clock on a Friday afternoon, and the Mannes Orchestra rehearsal ended with our conductor, Carl Bamberger, a full-fledged living link to Viennese musical tradition, giving the cut-off to the final bar of the fourth movement of the First Symphony of Johannes Brahms. Rupert, my Austrian barfly, knew about Bamberger, the conductor who came to the States just before World War II with all the credentials and gravitas of Georg Solti, but never quite made his mark. We students at Mannes were the lucky recipients of luminous, heavy-accented eccentrics like Carl Bamberger.

Brahms's First was solidly in the muscle memory of my fingers. I knew it well from high school youth symphony concerts. That afternoon the symphony's resolution in C major was fitting, as the first trombonist played his key-defining arpeggio passage at the very end of the last movement. A solid and fixed *do:* the fundamental, most down-to-earth note of Western music, from the middle of the piano, from which all other tonality is defined. Hammered at, whacked at, until there could be no mistake. C major is the mother of all keys, at times generic but always a welcome landing place. Brahms had been just twenty-one when he began composing his First Symphony, and he took all of twenty-one years to complete it. I was not yet twenty-one.

On this particular afternoon I couldn't linger to chat with fellow students as we all packed up our instruments. David, a clarinetist with aspirations of becoming a conductor, tried to get my attention. He was a double major, studying conducting with Bamberger, and wanted to gather a wind group together for later that evening to read through Mozart's *Gran Partita*. That would have been lovely.

But I was in a hurry because I was in the middle of a cluster-noted, atonal, tone-row life, banging on a metaphorical piano like a toddler let loose at Steinway Hall—a child who couldn't hit middle C to save herself.

A few years before I met Don G., "someone" had been "hurt"—or so his story went when he'd let the beans out one evening. The time had come for him to explain why I wouldn't be seeing him quite as often for a while. I'd accepted his cursory explanation on its shiny, hot surface. "Hurt" sounded reasonable: it bounced easily, a dull pain, or a weak throb. Exactly what *kind* of hurt was information I did not want lingering in my sensitive and attuned ears.

But on that Friday afternoon as the rehearsal ended, a generic hurt would actually have sufficed, because I was about to spend the next twenty-one Saturdays visiting Don G. at Rikers Island jail, where he was doing time to pay for the hurt he caused.

I quickly threw my oboe in its case, rushed out of the re-hearsal hall, and headed down to Greenwich Village to meet Don G.'s mother, a doyenne of the art world. I slipped into a hard Vienna café chair opposite her in an Italian restaurant called

Gene's on 11th Street just off Sixth Avenue. She'd called the day before to arrange this meeting to discuss the issue of the day— her son's incarceration. As I sat down I saw her smile, an expression I didn't understand.

"Marcia, I know this is all a shock.... We are all *terribly* shocked. But you have to keep this buttoned up. For *Steve.* We need you to just wait this out, and then when he gets out, we can discuss the next steps."

I took in this refined woman; a pillar of society she was. And also intent on my silence.

"Okay."

I didn't know her well, having met her only a few times over the past year. She and her husband were art patrons, owning works by Picasso and Klee and Miró and Nevelson, and had donated multimillion-dollar works of art to the Met and MoMA. Maybe they'd rubbed elbows with Mrs. S. before she moved to Boston. Her exclusive world was small and closed ranks quickly; she'd made that clear.

The waiter brought her a white wine and me a Coca-Cola. The sugar immediately eased my headache as she plodded on with her smiling pep talk.

"Because we know how much you care for him, and he *certainly* thinks a great deal of you."

"I know."

"And the last thing Steve needs is for this to get out. It would really spoil things for him...and hurt him. And *you, too,* of course."

That smile again.

"Okay."

"Because this is all so terribly hard on his father and me. You understand."

"Yes."

"So, dear, let us know if you need anything at all. And we'll all just get through this together. It's what we'd *prefer*."

"Okay."

Hunker down and practice the oboe and make visits and keep secrets. That is what any reasonable family, of *any* station in life, would prefer.

The waiter dropped the plates on the table. She had fillet of sole. I ate a club sandwich with french fries, for old times' sake. I didn't trouble her by asking her to divulge the ugly details of Don G.'s mightily defended incarceration or her son's penchant for guns.

When the meal was finished and our woman-to-woman negotiations were concluded, I pulled some money out of my purse.

"No, *no*, darling. Please: my treat. I have an account here. It's *nothing* to me."

"But it's *something* to me. I like to keep things even. I pay my own way."

"As you wish; whatever you prefer."

The smile had evaporated.

Walking the ten blocks uptown to my apartment on Seventh Avenue, fresh from dinner, I knew I would sleep a hard-fought slumber. My headphones were ready to assume the position, delivering the "Liebestod" to bolster my courageous silence.

I dropped to my bed. Suddenly my entire body hurt with a pain I'd not remembered for a long while. It was a memory of a coughing-up, searing agony that spiked from my toes through my pelvis to the very ends of my hair. The memory of slashing smiles and my father's grinding lessons on how his family prefers to maintain silence. Pushing Kirsten aside, I grabbed Brahms's First from my stack of records and dropped the needle at the end. I hastily downed four aspirins, chewing the last one, which got caught in my throat, and slept to the simplicity of C major.

The Q100

MOTHERS—MOSTLY MOTHERS—WIVES, children, and various other relations accompanied me to Rikers Island the next day. I woke earlier than I needed to and was raw with a buzzed and jagged fatigue. Sitting near the front of a packed Q100 bus, I kept to myself, aware that the other passengers might be ruminating on what had brought me on this bus. Or perhaps that was just my privileged musing. I dared to look around and quickly averted my eyes when I caught a glance or two.

I saw large extended families determined to make an outing of the day, maintaining festivity for the sake of the kids, young ones and teens who might be visiting an uncle, a brother, a father. A boyfriend. Sound waves of emotions rose and fell— laughing followed by the swift, sobering quiet that descended when, I imagined, our destination was suddenly remembered. These sound amplitudes riding on wild emotions created a strange and angular melody, like a newly conceived musical genre composed by the justice system just for our bus, the Q100. For everyone, the trip was baldly public and yet heartbreakingly private.

Being made to wait at Rikers felt abusive and punitive, as

if we visitors were as guilty as the incarcerated. I was searched twice for contraband. Female guards pulled at my arms to twist me around during their search, and I remembered Whitney and David and how I had tugged at them just a year before, when I needed to get their attention, or just to be mean. My breath remained shallow throughout the day; I couldn't get a full lung of air. Breathing felt sharp, my lungs poked by the new spoke on my wheel.

He was sober. That is the clearest tiny detail I remember of the first visit. We took our sixty minutes greedily, talked very little, cried often. Then it was over, and I reversed the process, almost as if playing a tape backwards, with sounds resembling strange, up-inflected whooping. The security checks, then to the Q100 bus, to the subway, to my apartment, to my Kirsten. To sleep.

I had a church job to play the next morning.

That was the thing about being a girl who played the oboe and had a boyfriend in the clink. It was easy for me to separate the two realities and carry on as if all were harmoniously blended. This particular job felt like a gift: a Sunday morning service at the Abyssinian Baptist Church in Harlem at 138th Street and Adam Clayton Powell Jr. Boulevard, the Reverend Dr. Calvin O. Butts III at the pulpit. A violinist I knew hired a small orchestra, on occasion, to accompany the choir on hymns and to perform light classical pieces. This was becoming a regular gig.

The next morning, the 1 train emerged from the uptown tunnel and elevated itself at 122nd Street, where Manhattan dipped down and exposed its innards temporarily. Every single car was tagged by massive, puffy graffiti, not yet appreciated as the important art movement and political statement it would become. It was a crime of beauty.

The subway doors opened at 137th Street and Broadway, splitting someone's tag in two, and let me out into a very different, somehow less bright, world. Rikers had not yet left my bloodstream; I still ached from all the hours of sitting the previous day, on the bus and then on the chairs at the jail. Now I walked the few blocks to the church, stiffly, slowly; a white girl getting a few stares from astonished, well-meaning folks.

The church was always festive, and I needed a big crowd scene this particular Sunday, one like *Aida*'s "Triumphal March," where all the senses are stimulated: color and high drama. The hats worn by the ladies were almost as elaborate as a Carmen Miranda cornucopia, but instead of fruits they had flowers and wisteria cascading down to their shoulders.

Over the past Sundays, the Reverend Butts had impressed me. His sermons were a mixture of good solid advice with some brimstone thrown in. Although I didn't believe in God, when the Reverend Butts put his sermon solidly on the pulpit, I was converted. There was even something for the nose. The smells coming from the basement of the church pervaded the entire sermon: lots of coffee and soul food for the social gathering afterward. By the end of the two-hour service, a strong body odor pushed through as well. Soul *and* body were involved if you wanted to worship the Lord properly.

As the sermon began, the Reverend Butts gradually delivered his A game. I settled back in my chair within the orchestra, listened to the smoldering embers in his voice, and for the first time in about forty-eight hours, since the downbeat of the Brahms symphony at Mannes, I took a deep breath. The sermon, the music, the hymns in C major with godlike plagal cadences, and the few hours of distance from Rikers finally allowed me to release some tension.

There came a point in the Baptist service when the Reverend Butts asked the worshippers to take a moment to wish peace to those around them. Voices bubbled up with peppered *p*'s from the repeated word: *Peace*. I figured I'd jump on the bandwagon, inspired by my gradually lifting mood. Now the church jostled with a few minutes of quiet activity, our rapt attention temporarily broken with the reverend's blessings. We were grateful to get up and move and wish each other peace.

A woman made her way up from the back of the church. She was fanning herself. Her lavender chiffon dress blew back as she walked, and a modest hat of flowers was perched at a stylish angle, hiding her face. A bosom of pearls. In her arms clung a small girl, about three years old, similarly dressed to the nines. I noticed the woman weaving her way down the aisle, deftly dodging the other peace-wishing parishioners who had spilled out into the aisles.

As if pushed by an invisible and breezy locomotion, the string players parted to let her through the orchestra. She was bound my way. And she took my hand.

"Peace to *you*, my sister."

I reeled back on my heels and sat down heavily. *Busted.* From Brahms to Rikers to the Lord. She, too, had been on the Q100 bus the day before.

Steve came home from jail, twenty-one Saturdays in, a docile man. Sobriety lasted just two weeks. With a belly full of ouzo and drug-induced pep, he arrived at the apartment and set to vacuuming my carpet with earnest intention. As he rocked the Hoover about, I lay on the sofa, pointing to the areas he'd missed. If he was going to be my mother, at least he could do her bang-up job. Fresh from jail, he was now, it seemed, a stickler for housekeeping.

A few days after he pulled the Hoover out of my closet, I decided I was tired of Don Giovanni's composite burlesque of my mother and my father. I called a friend and asked him to help me box up all Don G.'s stuff in my apartment and bring it to the 11th Street family town house. We hailed a cab I could not afford, loaded up the trunk, and sped down Seventh Avenue. The maid answered the door. We shoved the boxes, clinking with glass pieces, over the threshold. Steve could chew it all in hell.

23rd Street

THE SUN WAS bright, too bright to look at, so I kept my head down and stared at the uneven, pebbled sidewalk. Cigarette butts, a Dunkin' Donuts wrapper, a well-flattened coffee container. My bare neck absorbed the August sun's rays: maybe I would be found with a badly sunburned and slightly mangled neck.

That day in late August, after my graduation from the Mannes College of Music, I felt the cars whiz by me; sensing their speed, I wondered which would be the one. Standing still just outside the Angry Squire restaurant at the corner of 23rd Street and Seventh Avenue, I set my legs slightly apart, as Kirsten might have stood onstage singing the "Liebestod." And I observed and calculated. It was broad daylight, about noon. I mused about the perfect car. Just one seemed easy and reasonable, not too messy.

My parents attended exactly two concerts in my entire career as a musician. The first of these bookends was my senior graduation recital at Mannes two months before. After that concert, Adelweird had birthed me out to the New York City freelance scene, and throughout the summer after graduation, I began to get some work. Still, to keep body and soul together, I held down the financial fort at the restaurant, working five nights a week. I put up a good front. But underneath I was listless and aimless, missing Don G., sleeping a lot, always practicing and questioning everything. There were no answers…but there was a solution.

My mental checklist was now exhaustive and complete. There would be me, the car, the person in the car, and debris from the crash. I imagined that not too much damage would be done to the driver, who might suffer only bruises or a broken bone at the most. But I didn't want to dwell on that, selfish victim that I was. I just needed to ensure my own death. As I stood at the curb, weighing every last note of the final act of my Chelsea opera, I figured that when the right car sped along, I would know it instinctively.

The cars passed by, the pedestrians dodged me, and some sent me a sidelong irritated look, because I was standing right in their way. Clearly hindering the progress of the world at that point, I resolved to get on with it.

Just as I was revving up to leap, I sensed a woman watching just offstage, at the edge of my sight line. *Oh, who cares?* I thought. Let her gawk at the car wreck on Seventh Avenue. I quickly stepped off the curb toward my intended car, and simultaneously she rushed over and pushed me down hard onto the street. My arms splayed as an instinctive protection (funny, that); I skittered about five feet forward on my stomach, with my limbs spread-eagled. My eyes got a close-up focus shot of a half-full box of Camels.

Strangers rushed to the woman, trying to contain her, thinking that she had attacked me. Actually, she *had*. She screamed, behaving more like a lunatic than even the suicidal girl now lying in the middle of the street.

"Don't you DARE do that again! Don't even think of it. I'll be watching you!"

People quickly backed away, assuming we must have known each other, and in about fifteen seconds it was all over. In dirty Chelsea, no one wanted to be involved in personal scuffles.

It was not personal. It was about as anonymous as it could be. I rose up off the ground and picked some cigarette butts off the sticky blood still sluicing down my gouged palms. We warily eyed each other for a few seconds. Then just as quickly, dismissing me as an unimportant nuisance, she turned on her heel and walked away. I retreated, furious that a total stranger had thwarted my well-considered attempt.

As I walked the few blocks downtown toward my apartment, pedestrians streamed past me. Now feeling exposed, I was careful not to make eye contact, imagining that people knew what I had just done. Before the pratfall, I felt so courageous and dead certain. Now I cringed at my weakness and my utter failure. And my shuddering sense of shame.

Bed, my old friend, beckoned. Wrung out, I headed for it, praying for some sleep. I was about to drift off when I heard the guy on the first floor screaming at his dog in their backyard garden. The whaps, as the guy hit the dog, jolted me awake. Quickly, I ran to my window and climbed out onto my fire escape. He and his belt were really going at it.

"You fucker! Get off that dog! I'm calling the cops right now."

"Mind your own business, you stinking bitch." That *word*.

The dog was now sitting quietly, docile, not even noticing the verbal sparring, and for a second I wondered whether I had dreamed the beating. The guy ran into his apartment, and in a few minutes I heard his rapid *tat-tat* steps up the stairs. He began pounding on my door with a hammer.

"I'm gonna fucking kill you, you bitch. I *know* this is your apartment. You're the one who plays that instrument!"

Sitting silently on my bed, I remained still as he continued to slam at my door. I had just tried to kill myself not an hour before, and now this guy was promising to finish me off. I considered letting him in just so he could give me the beating I surely deserved. I'd sit, docile, and take it, just like his dog.

My trusty headphones were sitting on the bed, and I stealthily wrapped them around my ears, dropped the needle, and turned up the volume. Lying down, with the hammer still beating away at my door, I listened and tried to synchronize the jolt of the punching hammer to the pulse of the music. It almost matched up, like two clocks ticking loudly and hitting the same tick every thirteen seconds or so. I was used to slapping sounds and an out-of-sync life. Now the music in my ears would mix it up and dissipate the rhythm. I managed to slip off to sleep in spite of the racket.

I woke up to some timid rapping on my door. The music had long since stopped, and my headphones had fallen off my head, landing on the carpet.

Walking to the door, I quietly tested my voice.

"Who's there?"

"It's Isabella, from the first floor. I want to explain. Please open up."

Having never spoken to this couple, I was surprised to hear a foreign accent. Maybe Italian. I cracked the door open and saw a very small blond woman standing there in her pajamas. This seemed safe. As I opened up, the first thing I looked at was the other side of my metal door. It was riddled with deep dings from his hammer. There must have been hundreds of them.

"Please. You must forgive my boyfriend. You see, the dog. He is the puppy. And he chewed up all Nathan's records. He has many of the LPs, and he came home and found they were destroyed. By the dog. You see. So he went a little crazy."

Sleep was mixing me up. The woman was so tiny and thin. An urgent thought sliced across my head—I had to get her and the dog away from that guy. But it subsided quickly.

Instead, I hissed: "Just tell that fucking maniac you call your boyfriend that if I *ever* hear one sound against that dog ever again, I'll call every agency in the city. And get yourself a new boyfriend. How can you *be* with someone like that?"

"He has his good points...."

"*Right.* I'm sure. Don't they all?"

I nodded at the hammered door, as if to press my case. My fingers went to the surface to feel the divots, and she saw my henna-colored, blood-caked hands, which I'd never bothered to wash when I walked in off the street a few hours before. In the garish light of the fluorescent-lit hallway, I must have looked like a ghoul from hell. Her eyes widened, then she turned and started down the stairs, her slippers flopping in rhythm.

Moments later, in the bathroom, I saw that my face was also streaked with blood, probably from restless sleep. Who was the real monster? Me, the bitch? Or that maniac on the first floor?

Big Boys

Fresh out of college, you get a call out of the blue from a big music contractor in the city who asks you to play second oboe for an orchestra concert. He had come to the end of his regular list of oboists and got your name from a violinist friend from Mannes. You'd auditioned for permanent positions in a few orchestras over the last year but had not done particularly well, and you're discouraged. But now you feel like jumping out of your skin. This is how they say it starts: a contractor gets your name, he calls you—taking a chance; you play well, you get called again for other jobs, and your career is launched, little by little, job by job. In a way, you feel like freelancing has picked you—an inevitable fate—and, happily, you go along for the ride.

But there's a catch: you need to join the union in order to be able to accept the job.

With money earmarked for your electric bill, you pay your very first union dues. A sickening feeling comes with handing over the money, but now you're guaranteed union-scale rates. Con Edison will just have to wait.

*Arriving at Carroll's on West 41st Street—an iconic re-
hearsal studio where all the big freelance orchestras rehearse—you see that it's actually fairly shabby-looking: just
a big, cavernous room with low ceilings. But wonderful playing fills it as musicians warm up. You walk in, mousy, young,
and possibly not up to the task, making your way to the first
row of the wind section. Everybody else, familiar with each
other, is chatting up a storm. Shy and a little sad, you realize this is a club you're not a member of yet. The men look
old, maybe fifty; the women look like they're your mother's
age. But when you observe more closely, younger faces appear
around shoulders and instruments, and inwardly this lifts
your morale just a bit.*

*You sit in the second oboe chair, next to the guy playing
first oboe. He's a god in the freelance industry: serious idol territory. You've met before through friends but have never played
together. His sound is pointed, brighter and different from
yours—but this is immaterial. He is simply a phenomenal
musician. Just by sitting next to him, you will surely learn
something pivotal.*

*Almost nonstop throughout the rehearsals, the principal
oboist makes witty, sardonic jokes about the conductor and
other colleagues. You feel immediately welcomed, in his corner. And he's so funny you can hardly play at times from
laughing so much. But when it comes to the music, he is
deadly serious, and this also puts you at ease. You are more
alike than dissimilar.*

*On the day of the concert, as you're warming up, the
principal oboist asks if you could take over a job for him
that he needs to get out of. He just got called for a better*

gig. This happens a lot among freelancers—jockeying for position and jobs—and it's another way a career in music gets started or propelled along. Of course you accept, which results in playing your very first performance at Carnegie Hall.

Clint

I WAS WIDE awake and particularly hell-bent. Still thinking of the compliant, tiny blond Italian girl in pajamas and floppy slippers, her beaten dog, cigarette butts, my newly scabbed palms, and the head of a hammer, much later in the evening I made my way down Seventh Avenue into the Village toward a bar called "The Local, Formerly the Locale."

The place was noisy and busy, with strong lighting that allowed for quick assessment upon entering. I scanned the bar area and took my stool in a dark corner toward the back. Jim, the bartender, was on duty: just the man I was looking for. I'd slept with him a few times since my breakup with Don G. and in a weak moment succumbed to lending him the two hundred dollars in cash I had tucked away in my apartment for emergencies. He'd stopped answering my repeated calls about paying me back, so occasionally I stopped into the "The Local," hoping to stake my claim on his upcoming paycheck or his nightly tips. Already in a craggy mood from my encounter with the guy wielding the hammer, I'd reached my limit and was generally sour on men.

Clint Eastwood walked up beside me. At least that's what my confused double take confirmed. Upon third inspection I saw that he was just a dead ringer. Settling in next to me, he ordered his drink from Jim.

Back to my relentless nagging, I slammed my fist onto the bar to get Jim's attention, startling Clint.

"When can you pay me back, Jim?"

"In a month, I promise."

"You said that six weeks ago."

"I know. But my brother's been staying with me, and I have to pay for him."

"That's not *my* problem! In the meantime, I have stuff to buy. You know—food? Clothes? Can't you just give me your tips from this evening?"

"I'll call you, I promise."

"Right."

Clint was obviously eavesdropping on the unfolding scene, intrigued by the argument between a young white girl and a six-foot-six bearded black man.

He swiveled on his stool to face me, breaking the torque of the argument.

"What're you drinking? Can I buy you the next?"

"It's just club soda, but sure, why not?"

I was careful to keep my newly scabbed palms hidden. Bruce, his actual name, ordered another Drambuie, a sweet and potent liqueur just like ouzo, and my club soda. Grateful that someone was taking me off his back, Jim knocked twice on the bar: a signal that the drinks were on the house.

"I don't want a free drink *by the way!* I'd rather have the money! *Jesus!*"

I screamed it at Jim's back as he turned quickly away from us, grateful to be saved by a pseudo movie star.

"Are you two a couple?"

"I slept with him a few times.... He owes me money."

"You live nearby?"

"Chelsea."

"What do you do?"

"I play the oboe."

"Ah. What's that?"

"It's a musical instrument."

"You mean you play in an orchestra?"

"I wish."

Back and forth we chatted. Over the next hour, he eventually pried out of me the salient surface details of my life. Question after question; one thousand questions. I liked the attention, and it was easy to answer in the fewest words possible. Each short answer raised another question. For me, it was an exercise; for him, a trivia game. Jim just kept the free drinks coming.

"Do you make a living at it?"

"Why? Does that matter?"

"No. I'm just curious.... I don't know any classical musicians."

I sighed, exasperated at having to explain the facts of life to a musical neophyte.

"Okay. Look. I work as a waitress, but I also play some music jobs. More, lately. It's a balancing act."

"Don't you want to know what I do?"

"No."

"Are you always this cranky?"

I thought for a few seconds. Why *was* I being such a bitch?

"I'm sorry. So. What do *you* do?"

"None of your business."

We both laughed, breaking the tension.

"So you have to be pretty good to make a living as a musician."

"You think so?"

"Well, I'd presume that it's a pretty niche occupation. Are you any good?"

"That's what they tell me."

"What happened to your hands?"

I had loosened my grip on the glass and also on my vigilance. Examining my hands, I carefully considered my response. My attempt at death had been just that afternoon, but it felt like days had passed.

"Oh. I just fell this afternoon."

"Pretty nasty fall…you're still oozing blood."

He was right. The sweat from the glass on my club soda had moistened the caked blood on my hands. The bar napkin was bright pink with diluted blood.

"Whatever."

"Well, seriously, you should have your hands wrapped up. They'll never heal quickly if you keep using them this way."

"Jesus! I'm not a baby!"

"Well, don't bite my head off.…I'm just trying to help.…"

"I don't need your help. But you know how you *can* help? Just shut up about my hands and all your questions. Take me home and fuck me. That would help a *lot*. We've been wasting all this time here so you can figure out how to get me to that place where I say yes. Well. I'll just cut to the chase for you. I say yes very, very easily.… *You'll* see. Just ask Jim. He'll tell you: yes is my favorite word."

His eyebrows rose. After a few seconds he smiled that devil smile.

"Okay. You're the boss. Let's go."

We left the bar at 1:00 a.m. and stayed up well past dawn, closed up behind the metal door of a hundred dings. Bruce introduced me to my first taste of the racing, zippy, motormouthed, best-ideas-in-the-whole-wide-world drug, cocaine. Suddenly we were smart. Brilliant, even. There was so much to say and not nearly enough time to say it. The trick was to jam as many words as possible into a twenty-four-hour night. What a 180 for the tamped-down, somnolent girl who was spare with her words.

In between all the millions of words, we managed to slip in sex. The best sex, the kinkiest sex, the hardest-driving sex, legs-flying-in-the-air sex, every-which-way sex. We had the truest, bluest sex that two human beings had ever experienced or could even imagine.

In the lull of those rare deathly still moments, lying next to each other, molding our bodies together while face-to-face, we proclaimed our love over and over and over, with our voices directed straight into the other's airway—offering each other the breath of life. This hours-old love was intense and urgent and crazy and undeniably revolutionary. Then, when the birdies finally chirped, off to sleep.

This Mephisto-man, this rapid scene changer, demanded a new devil's pact. Married at New York City Hall after a few months of nonstop drugged dating, I let the oboe fall from my hands, bouncing to the ground. I became someone I didn't recognize—the devoted female lead in an opera called *Faust*.

Noise

That penetrating sound of Kirsten's love voice must have merged with the genetic makeup that had been stamped into your brain as a young girl, when you listened and heard what was unknowable at the time. It was hollow and echolike yet, paradoxically, fully filled out, spreading to the edges of her sound cavity. Her vocal vessel had no bottom, just the abyss. Her vibrato had an even quality to the amplitude, which left you feeling satisfied and, sometimes, oddly smug. You'd dive into that sound and wallow, spending a leisurely afternoon dozing in bed with the drapes drawn shut. No worries about time or whether it was day or night. Kristen kept you on a limp edge, at the wonderful cusp between awake and asleep. When she sang, things in your world were just about as right as they ever could be. Even as you lay on the carpet, four years old, a naive witness to her mystery.

Yet music is simply sound, or, more fundamentally put, noise. The rhythm of a hammer on a door. The distantly dulled slap to a dog's fur. The screech of a car braking too late. Or too soon. The oboe that has fallen off the face of your map. Now you want to banish all noise from the planet earth. And Kirsten's voice?

You want to scrub her DNA from your skin with a rough, violent rasp. It's all just noise: some damned tremulous volcanic connection that's erupted, leaving a messy flow of hot lava that you need to quickly sidestep.

Gato

THEY COULDN'T LIFT her head because she had been intubated, so the nurses had just plaited her hair down the sides. She looked like Heidi, yodeling on the Alps. Taut braids started dark brown at her skull, and then, about two inches down, where her dye line began, Heidi emerged, turning platinum. Peering into her face, I tried to discern some kind of movement or awareness. Her eyes were swollen shut, the lids violet-blue, with shallow veining and goopy stuff crusted around the slits.

And she was skinny; so lean and sweet. She really was a thin-boned girl after all. I'd always taunted Jinx for being the fat sister. But here she was, revealing her true delicate, waiflike frame. In a coma. On life support. Denuded of all pretense and bravura.

I reconnected with my runaway sister a few months after I married Mephisto. I'd seen her, upright and chattering, just a few weeks before at Palsson's, a restaurant-bar on West 72nd Street. Jinx sold us cocaine from time to time.

Three o'clock in the morning at Palsson's seemed to drag the life stories out of anyone. Gato Barbieri played "Europa" in what seemed to be a continuous loop on the jukebox, the perfect heartache music for punching regret or hope out of the best of the bar patrons. Ron, the bar manager, told his rubbed-raw tale of saving his brother from a car crash. That brother now sat in a wheelchair at the back of the restaurant, appearing sanguine about his lot as a quadriplegic. Every now and again the owner, Stella Palsson, showed up, assessed the action, and quickly departed for destinations unknown.

My new husband recounted his own version of a life: working in London and Milan as the "youngest account executive for Young and Rubicam ever." I sat next to him, mute, smiling and high, as he regaled any dupe within earshot with sagas of driving around the shores of Lake Como, in Italy, at one hundred miles per hour with his friend Ahmed.

We were living off his hefty severance package from Y&R in an apartment on West 73rd Street just off Riverside Drive. When we returned home from our Palsson's postmidnight adventures, I walked into the apartment, knowing what must be done. Mephisto would sleep. But for the first time in my life, I could not bring sleep on without help. On the pretext of fetching a glass of water, I snuck into the kitchen to forage under the sink, where I hid the antidote for my molar-grinding cocaine buzz. Vodka—the original sneak's see-through booze. Blending in nicely alongside the cleaning supplies, or simple H_2O, it overrode the coke. My balancing act was well calculated: I chugged hard and deeply, and within ten minutes was so out of it I could not be roused until 1:00 p.m. the next day. My best state of being now was not listening to music or playing the oboe. I was in top form when I was tipping precariously into the land of Dead to the World.

It was clear what my Mephisto needed from me. He never smoothed out our wrinkled marital map neatly on the table, but

I knew our weak point was all about my talent, which seemed to punch him in his solar plexus. So my oboe, the ever-compliant third party, made a gallant and gracious retreat: first it lay on a desktop, unopened, staring me down daily. Then it backed onto a high shelf in a closet while I dug deeper into this marriage and committed myself more fully to a Mephistophelian version of love and happiness. Just as the devil planned, I dropped out of the music scene, at first showing up occasionally for the odd gig. Then, quickly, even those receded into the far-off horizon as my oboe began to gather dust on the floor of a closet I never opened.

Fighting was another clause in our marital contract. An abrasive energy pulsed between us, particularly when slivers of the bright light of day jabbed, unwanted, across our morning vision. I never actively participated in these fights, taking the complaints and the occasional backhanded swat—like Ali in his later years, backed against the ropes. A rope-a-dope who never fought back. There was no possibility of a reasonable truce with this devil.

Once in a while, my old self tried to reenter the ring, the old urge breaching the surface.

"I feel like I should practice today. It's been a while; I can't even remember how long. I need to get back into shape."

"Why?"

"Well, what if somebody calls me for a job? I need to sound good."

He roughly took me by the shoulders, pointing me to the front door, away from the closet where the oboe lay sleeping on the floor.

"Let's go get a drink. You can practice later."

Then I got the call from my mother about Jinx.

Having tried to end her life with pills, she lay in a coma and on a respirator at Bellevue Hospital. I quietly sat at her bedside, watching for movement, trying to imagine what it was like to be so unconscious that you couldn't even breathe for yourself. At first glance, I'm sure I looked like a concerned sister. Just below this thin veneer was the aching desire to be right where she was—not asleep but gone. For the first time in my life I envied my sister and her pumped diaphragm: in and out, steady as a funeral march.

The doctors kept strictly to business and were not sure of Jinx's prognosis. She might get off the respirator but still be a vegetable; or perhaps she might gain consciousness but have some brain damage. The nurses were simply angels, making sure that her hair was newly plaited every day, swabbing the yellow goop from her eyes in case she might open them and try to see. Jinx had slammed-shut eyes. She did not want to see.

They didn't come to see her every day, but when my parents did show up, my father wisely lurked in the background. On the fifth day, I noticed him standing at the end of a long hallway, holding a telephone book attached to the wall with a chain. Scribbling something on the wall, he let the heavy book drop from his hands when he saw me approach. It swatted down, smacking almost to the floor. Hundreds of phone numbers—the diner around the corner, the local pharmacy, private numbers for people perhaps now dead—had been written in haste on the roughly plastered wall.

"What are you looking for?"

"Oh, just browsing."

"In a telephone book?"

"Well, I was looking up some stuff, just trying to be prepared, you know."

"For what?"

"Coffins."

"Coffins?"

"Right, in case—"

Before Wotan, with his perfect Chiclet teeth, could complete his thoughts on the inevitable future for his close-to-death daughter, I grabbed the huge New York City telephone tome. Feeling the heft of eight million phone numbers and the hard binder cover protecting the thin pages from other grieving family members, I threw it down the hall as hard as I could. The ripping effect took plaster and all the dead people's numbers with it.

"At least wait until she's *dead*."

His eyes wandered to the ceiling; he had been caught, sheepish. The orderlies walked on by. It was business as usual at Bellevue.

As if jostled by the brutality of that off-pitch interaction, the next day Jinx woke up: a sobering miracle to all who witnessed it. Now dozing, she lay on her back with arms hanging down at the sides of the hospital bed, her fingers tickling in her sleep, perhaps from an amusing dream. I gingerly pulled the sheets up to her neck, smoothing out the wrinkles. Then I placed her arms back onto her midsection, with her hands on top of one another. She looked proper, almost regal, and I hoped that she was ready to face the world when she woke up again. Her bed was well made, fit for her next chapter of living. I stepped back, watching her now unaided sleep—without tubes or pump—admiring how clever she really was, and began to assess her suicide attempt with a fresh, discerning eye.

Jinx's naturally sleeping face glowed, slightly enlivened by her new consciousness. As for me, that time on 23rd Street had clearly been a warm-up. I needed act 2. This time, I would let *fate* do its mysterious dirty work.

In the late 1970s Central Park was not a nice place to be, even during the day. People certainly didn't dare take their final 9:00 p.m. dog walks in Central Park. Just a few blocks over, in the middle of human activity, the 72nd Street subway station pulsed with danger, abutting Verdi Square—more commonly known as Needle Park by those in the know. Palsson's was just down the street, after all.

With Jinx discharged from the hospital, thin but now upright, I was free to begin my own push. On four consecutive nights, I walked deep into Central Park, far enough so that I felt well isolated. Now I was ready to be attacked. My feet dragged a bit, still uncertain about what I really wanted from this dangerous stroll. Outwardly, I was a nonchalant young woman who just happened to be walking in the dark at one in the morning in a remote area of New York City.

One night the moon was out and full, and I looked up to watch the branches of the trees wave against the yellow orb. Then looking down, I urged my pupils to adjust to the black again. After peering carefully, I managed to make out the blades of grass on the ground, maybe even an ant or two strolling with me. Looking up and looking down seemed a good way to pass the time, like sightseeing in pitch black, straining for clarity.

Various benches presented themselves to me. I sat with eyes closed and willed myself to ease up and become disoriented as to where I was, east or west, north or south. Feeling momentarily directionless, I eventually gave in to the simple urge all living beings have—to know exactly where they are—and opened my eyes to scan the distance for the familiar double towers of the San Remo at 75th Street and Central Park West. They blinked with light and life. Only then did I know exactly where I was: waiting for something or someone to end or just divert the current trajectory of my life.

Stabbing. Rape, then bludgeoning. Gunshot. I mused on each potential future event, after which I might die quickly or I might survive. My uncertain and passive meandering must have been mistaken for a determined and defiant march, because people did walk by. But no one bit; no one even looked. I walked out each night, defeated. Saved.

Saved

My ambivalence about continuing to breathe persisted. After the four nighttime strolls, I plodded through the next week, repeating my marital drug-and-sleep schedule. On the seventh day, a Sunday morning, a miracle phone call came to me. An old friend from Mannes had made dozens of calls to fellow alumni and finally managed to track me down. It was David, the aspiring conductor. He was putting together a small chamber orchestra concert in a local church and needed a principal oboist.

The program was to include *Siegfried Idyll* by Richard Wagner. As we discussed this, my skin went wet with slick sweat, a visceral reaction that unnerved me initially but that I welcomed in the next second. I understood this to be a sign of relief—perhaps release. Written for the birth of Wagner's son, Siegfried, the music is relentlessly tender yet somehow heroic, reflecting the vulnerable and hopeful possibilities of love between two people and the potential for a new life.

"David, I'm not in shape, just so you know. I haven't played for quite a while." Someone had just offered *me* new life, and I was summoning the courage to say yes.

"I don't care, Marcia. You'll pull it together. I want your sound, especially in the Wagner. That's why I made all these damned phone calls!"

"Okay. You have no idea what you have done for me. But I'll take it."

"I don't know what you're talking about, Marcia....But the first rehearsal is in five days. Can you manage that?"

A familiar and almost painful stab pushed at me—for what I was about to do and for what I had almost given up. To play those notes; to hear those tight, dense chords; to feel alive through my own breath; and to touch, through my oboe and music, Wagner's love for his son and wife. This was a privilege I had roundly rejected for too long.

"I can manage. I'll be there."

Dropping the phone into its cradle, I walked over to the closet, knelt down, and pulled out the oboe. It was that fast and sudden. And *urgent*. Kirsten. She'd poked into the surface of my skin, like an old and fading tattoo getting freshly inked. Over the next four days, I played for hours and hours. Nonstop, it seemed. Going through dozens of reeds, trying to get into shape. Trying to recapture my sound, a sound that would do my Kirsten justice.

Mephisto stood back and picked his fights. I ignored his taunts. He was losing me to Kirsten, a woman he had never even met.

The church was on the East Side. On the night of the concert, I walked through Central Park, past the very benches and trees that were shrouded in black just two weeks before. I'd arrived early to warm up slowly, leisurely, without pressure. The audience trickled in, then filled the church; the echoing chatter died down as the program began with a Mozart overture, followed by Beethoven's First Piano Concerto.

Then it was time for me to take *Siegfried Idyll* in hand. Nervous, I hoped I could perform with the beauty required of a principal oboist. The orchestra was small, so my sound laid a specific color onto the composite resonance whenever I had an entrance. As the orchestra wove itself through me, I felt a deep jolt from Wagner's signature harmonic language. So very familiar yet distant: like an old friend recounting a family story I'd known since I was four years old.

The grounding motif of rocking triplets played by the French horns called to me, over and over. Implied in the silent first triplet was a sound that wanted to come through: inevitable. And I was gently buffeted back and forth in the calm yet deep chasm that was reorganizing my shaky world, all inside the tight sphere of this orchestra.

For those two hours, I did not need to be deeply unconscious. My guts dropped down, and the cogs turned over and clicked in, newly oiled by this music. I felt awake and alive with the backstage specter of Kirsten, the prescient savior who'd resurfaced from the deepest part of my deadened heart. She had always been there, spending time on the other side of the earth. My orbit realigned: I was a musician again.

I bit the worm and called Pete, Sal, and Duane from the Village restaurant. They were six-foot-by-two-foot slabs of pure muscle and heart and agreed to help me move out. Mephisto stood back, literally shaking with rage. His oboe-player experiment was over; that lass had fallen lifeless on the grassy midnight grounds of Central Park and in the drab hallways of Bellevue Hospital. With one hundred dollars in my pocket, I took almost nothing with me. As long as I could play the oboe, I would be okay.

Kirsten sang:

Sweet breath
softly wafts—
Friends! Look!

Sound

Your sound, distinctive among New York players, has become
something of a calling card. Oboists arrive early for rehearsals,
needing to fully warm up in order to play the tuning A for the
rest of the orchestra. Through the years, other musicians men-
tioned that they knew who was playing the oboe well before
seeing you. As they came down the stairs from the Carnegie Hall
dressing rooms onto that stage or into any rehearsal studio in
town, your signature sound preceded your face. It was that dis-
tinct and unusual. They described it as European, German. You
think of it as just emerging from your heart.

If you don't love your sound, it hampers your ability to spin
music the way you imagine. Sound is like a fingerprint to musi-
cians. To fully and freely express music with commitment, your
sound must reside deep in a corner pocket, like a cube of sugar
left on the tongue to disintegrate in its own time. You have a
sound ringing in your ears all day every day that cannot be si-
lenced. It is your essence—your soul turned inside out, exposing
you for the world to notice, scrutinize, and perhaps love.

Gato Redux

In 1982, living a post-Mephistopheles life in a sublet on West 70th Street tasted like a bittersweet concoction of welcomed solitary confinement and endless loneliness. I had everything I needed, living in the furnished apartment of an actor on the road for a year with a touring musical. I took great comfort from my oboe and Kirsten, always on call in my headphones. Spot, my lucky black cat, although still showing signs of trauma from the rough removal from her equally rough home, quickly made her nest inside the coat closet, curling herself up in a tight, protective ball. But after the first few weeks, she gradually ventured out to laze on the bed with me, watching the pigeons on the windowsill overlooking 70th Street. We spent hours examining their lovely cooing life. I could be a pigeon and enjoy that underrated perching life. But Palsson's was down the street, and Gato was playing nightly. And Gato's jukebox "Europa" beckoned with long, sinewy arms.

About a month into my newly single seclusion, curiosity came sniffing. That evening I'd ordered a curry dinner in and was feeling sated and content and very safe. Safe enough to wonder about all the people I knew from my late nights at Palsson's. Ron and Stella, for example: they'd been my built-in 3:00 a.m. social life, and I was curious.

I heard him—Gato—wailing away before I even opened the door to Palsson's. Ron, at the back of the restaurant, vaguely nodded to me. Like a junkie, I gave in to temptation, and as my eyes got accustomed to the smoky air, I began scouting for connections—both personal and maybe even medicinal. Once I'd settled myself at the bar with a club soda, a woman I vaguely remembered walked over and offered me a Quaalude. Sure. I accepted the pill and took half, pocketing the other side.

I was not a typical drinker or drug user. I was the cheapest of dates, high even before booze kicked into my blood—one drink would slide down my gullet to leave me instantly weak-kneed. And cocaine was always just a vehicle to drive me to a place of chatty connection with people. These were the accomplices I required to imagine identifying this "love" thing. To pick it out of a lineup: *Ah! So that's it. That's what they're all talking about!* And for the short time I was with Mephisto, this combination—alcohol and cocaine—seemed to be a raging late-night success. Curious and lonely now, I had been nostalgic for that perfect synthesis of gossamer edginess when I walked out the door of my apartment and headed toward Palsson's.

Gato played on. A well-dressed couple approached. His shoes: a shiny patent leather. Her lipstick: much too red. She struck up the chatter.

"Hi. Are you a regular?"

"No; not really. I used to come in a lot, but this is the first time in about a month."

"We just saw a show and then had dinner downtown. We're staying at the Excelsior."

"Oh?"

I turned and looked them up and down. It was curious they were telling me all this: not the typical anonymous chitchat in a bar.

"It's a pretty dingy place, actually.... We were expecting a bit more."

"Well, it attracts mostly Europeans who can't afford the Plaza." I knew the Excelsior Hotel, on West 81st Street, myself, because I'd stayed there a few times when Mephisto and I were at particularly nasty odds and I needed an overnight safe house.

They were silent, not knowing if my comment was a put-down or a disguised compliment on their international élan. Their accents revealed their homeland: New Jersey. Rubes from the countryside.

"You seem loopy. Did you take something? Or is it just the booze?"

My head jerked back in reflex. This was also unusual—to call out someone's drugged look. They *were* novices. But about an hour into my half Quaalude, I went along with it.

"I took half a Quaalude. Just relaxing."

"Oh. Well, we have something to help with that. Want some?"

"Sure."

They slipped a glassine packet to me under the bar along with a short, cut-off straw. Off to the ladies' room I sauntered, smug and self-assured, hoping to counter the Quaalude's loopy effect with some free coke.

About ten minutes later, back at the bar chatting with my new friends, I felt a roiling of nausea come up, very fast and intense. Knocking some chairs over, I ran for the bathroom and jammed myself into an empty stall, my head over the toilet. The curry dinner came up, all orange with bits of spinach floating to the top. Sliding down onto the floor next to the toilet, panting and waiting for the next wave, I broke into a fierce sweat that soaked right through my blouse. I retched for what seemed like an hour, but it could have been just ten minutes.

The Jersey woman came back and helped me up. My feet felt bottomless, with the contrary sensation of no floor beneath them.

"I see you're a novice. It hits people that way sometimes with the first blow."

"What do you mean? What the hell *was* that?"

"Heroin."

With my arms around her neck, and me bandy-legged, she danced me back to my bar stool. Together they got my bar tab paid and stuffed me into my coat. Out on the sidewalk, the fresh air was not helping much. I staggered to the curb and, leaning against a car, bent over to vomit again but heaved up nothing. The man asked where I lived.

"Oh. Just around the corner. But I'll be okay."

"No, no, no! We want to make sure you get there. Come on…let's just go."

Not in a position to resist or even walk, I put myself in their hands. Down the street we all walked, arm in arm in arm—old pals, it would seem. The man took the keys out of my purse to unlock the front door of the brownstone. We tag-teamed up the three flights and fell into the apartment. Spot made a dash for the hall closet.

It felt normal and sweet and very kind. They said they would take care of me, and I wanted that. I wanted friends, and in my dazed mind, they became the best of friends—at least for that long, zigzagging walk to my apartment.

Then the evening became a swirl of small resistances and gentle acceptances, each of which floated up and down, according to the heroin's whim. My impressions held moments of sharp focus before panning back for a gauzy long shot.

As I succumbed, almost happily, to passive sex with her, he remained in the background, pacing back and forth, his reflective shoes glinting in the lamplight. Looking for something, or just looking at us on the bed—a voyeur, maybe. His head zoomed in for a close-up more than once. I felt my eyelids being pulled back as he assessed my state. I couldn't move or didn't want to. Maybe I was smiling; I thought I saw him smile back. His movements were fluid and continuous as he roved the living room, me in a four-legged puddle with her. I allowed her to love me and pushed down the questions swirling in my brain: Is this okay? Is this what I want?

Heroin was doing its damnedest to show me a different version of letting go. I was not unhappy. With the help of this new and awful drug, I was a willing prisoner, not wanting to shake clear the lovely film that encased my mind. Except for the vomiting, it wasn't all that bad. These people were not evil, just strangers. In fact, they were the sweetest of strangers. After all, they had walked me home.

Daylight—two o'clock in the afternoon: the door to my apartment was slightly ajar, and Spot was trying her best to look through the cracked opening. I was lying alone on the sofa, somehow in my clothes but not the same clothes as the night before. A blanket had been neatly tucked over my legs. My feet poked out at the bottom of my body and seemed very far away. I noticed my socks were on upside down, with the heels at the top of my feet. As I tested getting up, my diaphragm muscles seized from throwing up all night. Feeling a need to pee, I couldn't make my legs move to get up off the sofa. My arms collapsed as I tried to lift myself up, and I fell back down to sleep.

Four o'clock in the afternoon: I came to with a start this time. Spot sat very close to my head, right on my chest, dozing and moving in sync with the rise and fall of my breathing. This was her usual destination when she wanted food: my chest. But the front door was closed now. Someone from the building must have shut it. Not wanting to disturb Spot, and afraid to reawaken the pain in my midsection, I turned my head to look around. The living room appeared in order.

My eyes focused in and out; I was not yet in control of my pupils. I settled my gaze on an object in the middle of the floor about two feet from me. This seemed to be the optimal distance for me to get my visual bearings. I stared. As I looked, confusion set in. What *was* that thing? The rectangular box was carefully wrapped in a pillowcase, tightly bundled, as if ready to be shipped off in the post. A curiosity. My head started to clear, and I began to study it. Gently releasing Spot to the floor, I reached down to pick it up and set it on my belly. With a quick intake of breath, I knew immediately what it was: my oboe. Wrapped in a pillowcase.

Now I was afraid. Adrenaline jammed into every inch of my body as I shot up from my prone position onto my feet. I ran to the bathroom, urgently needing to evacuate. My abs felt very tender, as if I had been punched. At the sink, water encouraged and braced me, and I lapped it up through my cupped fingers. Glancing into the mirror, I saw her red lipstick smeared all over my face. It was thick and everywhere. My ruby scarecrow face sickened me almost as much as the wrapped oboe, and I heard myself begin to whimper.

I returned to the sofa after washing my face and rocked back and forth with Spot rubbing around me, flicking her tail in my face. Slowly, the next, more intense level of fear knocked me back. Not for my personal safety but for the one thing in life I could not replace: my oboe.

I discovered telltale signs of theft. They had left my keys, so I felt some pretense of security. But a few pieces of jewelry were missing, including a watch that my grandmother had given me. About a hundred dollars in cash that I'd hidden in some socks in the very back of a dresser drawer were gone. They had left some rings that had little value. I couldn't figure it out.

Throughout that evening, as the heroin left my body and the haze lifted, I took several showers and examined my body for any marks—some sort of road map for what might have occurred over the course of those eight hours or so: maybe a bruise or a sore area. I determined that the man had not penetrated me, or at least I sensed he hadn't.

But I was a damned lucky trickster. My oboe was intact, with the reeds still in their zipper case: untouched, unharmed. And clearly ready to be stolen. Over the next few weeks I instinctively made a little ritual for myself. Whenever I left the apartment, I wrapped the oboe in the same pillowcase, in exactly the same way, placing it in the exact same location on the floor, not wanting to break the spell that I imagined had been cast upon me.

Cracked open, raw and vulnerable, I reached out to the most remote person in the solar system: my mother. And why not? I had a lucky oboe. I was a lucky girl. Maybe she would join me in my new aura.

My mother sounded tired when she answered my call. I assumed she was tired of the way I portrayed myself to her: a young—yet ancient—twenty-five-year-old soon-to-be-divorced daughter. Maybe she'd had enough of her daughters: their suicide attempts (known and unknown) and their abortions (known and unknown), their professional successes and personal failures, their husbands and boyfriends. I was just three months free of my marriage, and the shame of my sordid lifestyle with Mephisto kept me tightly bottled up. As with my relationship with Don G., I had revealed nothing to her, and she was never curious about any of it. Could I pique her interest now? As mothers go, she was still tantalizing to me, and I hung on to a vestige of hope that I might get under her skin—our skin—and graft us together. Then I would know that "this was it."

An Omelet

I MET MY mother for lunch at my favorite restaurant—Elephant & Castle. A cozy spot with great omelets and salads, it was pure Greenwich Village. I ordered my usual omelet with goat cheese and basil. She ordered the American omelet. Surely this venue would impress her and pry her open a bit. I was aching to feel even an infinitesimal mother-daughter connection.

"So, honey. How's everything going? Are you getting some jobs on the oboe? You know, your father and I will always pay for Katie Gibbs if you want."

She was at it already. I closed my eyes and counted to five. Opening them, I saw her diligently chewing her omelet, gazing over my head onto Greenwich Avenue.

"Things are going okay. I'm playing a bit."

"But not enough…"

"At the moment, no, not enough."

"Then what *about* Katie Gibbs?"

Five seconds.

"I'll pass on the Katie Gibbs. Actually I'm thinking of getting my master's in music. I think I can get a teaching fellowship, and they'll pay my way."

"Really? Is a master's *really* necessary?"

"Well, it'll give me some time to figure stuff out. You know…just some breathing room…now that…you know, I'm on my own."

"Well…whatever you think is best. Your father and I just always felt that a solid typing skill would be a good fallback for you."

"You're probably right…"

I took a deep breath.

"You know, Mom, I never told you what happened with Bruce."

"Happened? What do you mean?"

The waitress refilled our water glasses. My mother lifted her eyes over my head again: staring out the window, distracted by the presumably more interesting lives that passed us by on Greenwich Avenue.

"Well…you know…he, um…he used to hit me sometimes. Not a lot…but I had a black eye once. And it was kind of scary. You know. I just had to get out of there. And um…well…that's what happened.…"

The seconds pounded on, screaming in my head. I took a bite of my eggs and saw that her eyes never wavered from some object over my head, far off in her necessarily distant land. A blinding white disk appeared in front of my eyes, a sign that I might faint. I leaned into the front edge of the table.

"Well. I really can't talk about this now."

With those words, she pushed her half-eaten omelet forward on the table, stood up, shoving her chair back with the back of her smooth knees as she rose, and walked out of the restaurant. The composite motion was swift, deft, and complete. It looked rehearsed, as if she had done this before, perhaps many times. And of course she had. Whether on the phone or in person, I was still unable to pry apart the tight slats of fencing she used to protect herself from me.

The lump of eggs sat in my mouth. Minutes went by. The white disk faded. My heart slowed and my hearing returned. The goat cheese popped through, putrid and rancid. I swallowed. The waitress approached.

"Is everything all right?"

"Oh…yeah…ah…my mother just needed to leave. Can you wrap these omelets up for me to take home? I guess I'm finished."

I'd let the bomb drop: I had married a man just like her husband. We had both chosen muscular devil-men who hit women and girls, who had peculiar sexual predilections. She could not hear or acknowledge an iota of my pain, my story, or my life. She was done. Clearly tired and spent. I had held up a cracked mirror to her face, and I finally recognized what had been in front of *my* nose since I was four years old: I didn't know my mother at all. My *luck* had just run out.

Those omelets stayed in my refrigerator for weeks, lying like embryonic puppies wrapped in tinfoil. They stared at me daily as I mulled over what I would do with them, my lucky oboe, and my tired mother. Eventually they started to smell, and into the garbage they went. I cleaned the sublet and started looking for a new place.

Body Parts

He's already on top of you. He knows each nook and cranny of your being. He's whispering every scintillating bit of information you need to make your move. You take a breath and project your air. This maestro is God's gift to musicians. He uses his body parts to guide you and the world through this music.

Mahler's Sixth Symphony, the Tragic, *requires an enormous orchestra. You're sitting close to the brass section: eight French horns, six trumpets, four trombones, one tuba. The sound is overwhelming, and you have to wear earplugs for much of the big tutti sections.*

Just then, he really makes you crazy: he calls out to the sixth horn player during the loudest section imaginable: "Sixth horn, that's an E-flat on the second beat in that bar." Those ears. From God. Only a once-in-a-lifetime set of ears could hear that small discrepancy when the volume is so massive. You just adore those ears.

You get to a really delicate section where the music is quiet and tender; you feel like you're skating on a thin sheet of ice and could fall through a hole at any moment. The entrances are exposed and must be precise, and it's scary as hell. You're nervous.

But you look up and realize that he's got you covered. He sniffs. And with that tiny, minuscule sound that only the orchestra can hear, he gives you the exact placement of your scary entrance. That sniff. You could kiss that nose.

And don't get me started on his arms. His fingers tell you one thing, and later his elbows tell you something else. And when he uses the whole arm, it shows you something completely different. And he can change it up at will. Somehow, you just know what he wants. Nothing is in doubt, and nothing scares you. You love all his body parts.

The best part is that he never closes his eyes to you. You know that when a conductor closes his eyes while conducting, he is subconsciously afraid. Afraid that he will look at the whole orchestra staring back at him, and they will know that he is fearful. To face music, to understand it, to know it; this takes courage. There is no place for fear.

Tony

"*FLAWLESS!* PICK! UP!"

My curry dinner with mango chutney on the side sat on the warming table. Rushing in hungry, I was about to start my shift. The expediter, a guy named Jorge, loved to scream my nickname: Flawless.

After a day of classes at the Aaron Copland School of Music, where I was getting my master's in music, I had arrived at my new restaurant job on 57th Street and Sixth Avenue for the evening shift. One of around fifty servers, I was surrounded by actors, dancers, writers, and artists. Patrick O'Neal, the owner of the place and an actor himself, designed the work schedule to be flexible for employees who needed to attend auditions or classes. Patrick called me Flawless, and so, eventually, did all the staff and regular customers. I was a stern and, at times, downright mean waitress—but always with a smile on my face—demanding that my customers order in good time, not complain, and get out quickly. Turning tables and making money was my priority; efficiency my mantle. I wore my nickname like a badge of honor, because *that* was how I actually saw my life: clean and scraped down, pristine, free of fluff, with everything reduced to its essence.

Working at O'Neal's among creative people of all disciplines was a heady change from the small, insular Village restaurant. The New York Coliseum was around the corner, at Columbus Circle, and all the trade-show guys spilled into O'Neal's for drinks and dinner: the Thom McAn shoe guys, the Ralph Lauren guys, the Jordache jeans guys. Busy salesmen and busy waiters; the time flew, and we made money.

The Aaron Copland School of Music at Queens College fancied itself to be on a music conservatory level, but it was not quite there. Its academic emphasis was suited to music theorists, and I was required to take a few difficult theory classes I was ill prepared for. I limped along. My only obligation to the school, along with taking oboe lessons and a light load of class work, was to play in the school orchestra twice a week. In exchange, they offered me free tuition. Ronnie Roseman, my oboe teacher, gave me all the flexibility I needed. I knew exactly how I wanted to sound; Kirsten's voice still rang true in my ears. She continued to be my muse.

During the week, I arrived at Queens College at 7:00 a.m. after an hour-and-a-half commute by subway and bus. I'd find an empty classroom to practice in for two hours before classes or orchestra began. Then, at the end of the day, I began my reverse commute back into Manhattan and went on to my shift at the restaurant. I knew how to do this: I was an expert at discipline. Like a rubber band, my life was stretched as taut as it could go.

But I wanted a love life. Why not just tug a little more and snap back to a place I knew inside and out? My new love was a repeat: Don G.

Despite his prison record, drinking, gun toting, and glass chewing, I carefully reconsidered his endearing qualities. My grizzled barhopping boyfriend of yore was a respected glass-blower, a maker of both art glass and commercial objects, working out of his father's industrial glass factory in Queens. Well known in his field, he'd exhibited at the Corning Museum of Glass and the Toledo Museum of Art.

Pushing aside the potential for land mines, and inspired by the pristine memory of his art, I dove in for another chance. Our familiar love was just easier than a new, unknown devil.

"Hi, Tony."

"Marcia. *Jaysus.* What are you doing here? It's been, what, three years?"

The Village restaurant looked the same, save for a few new waitresses and a slightly different bar crowd. On a night off from O'Neal's, and after a full day of school, I was secretly hoping to see Steve.

Tony appeared miffed.

"Well, *that's* a nice welcome. Nice to see *you, too,* Tony...."

"I'm sorry. What can I get you?"

"Just a club soda. How's everything here, Tony? Where's Rupert? Is he still around?"

"Things are really kind of the same. But Rupert—he moved back to Vienna about a year ago. He really missed you when you disappeared. He was always talking about that singer you two were crazy about. Personally, it bored me to tears....That old lady Mary died. In her sleep, I think, thank the Lord. You remember her, right?"

I nodded, remembering that this elderly woman had had a huge crush on Tony and that he was terribly kind to her. Tony was a good bartender that way; he always dealt with his customers purely, without guile.

"That's about it for the news....You know how the bar business is. Booze levels everything out....But Marcia, what *happened?* You just never showed up for work one day. We were worried. Or at least *I* was."

Ah. *That* was it: I never said good-bye to the man who cared about me. The Irish never forget. I'd never considered his feelings, and I was about to abuse him again.

"Well, it's a long story. But I got married and divorced."

"Whoa. Please don't tell me Steve."

"*God,* no. Somebody else."

Tony stared at me, awaiting further explanation as to who the lucky bridegroom had been. When it didn't come, he busied himself cleaning glasses. Looking out the window for a few seconds, I dragged my eyes back to his. *Get on with it.*

"Tony. Have you seen Steve at all? I know he moved somewhere. Has he been in? I'm kind of curious what happened to him."

Tony stopped polishing. Our momentum of nostalgia halted dead on the tracks. He faced me.

"Marcia, no. *C'mon!* I warned you then, and I'm gonna to say it to you now. He's dangerous—and what the fook're you doing even *asking* about him? I was hoping you got all that shite out of your system. So no. I've not seen him. Okay?"

Not surprised by his vehement protest, I started in on the weakest defense of a lifetime.

"It's not like that...."

"No? Well, then, how exactly *is* it?"

"Please, Tony. I just want to talk to him. Do you have any idea where he might be?"

"Oh, fer fook's *sake.*"

He took the Manhattan phone book out from behind the bar and with a grand gesture slammed it down in front of me. The other bar patrons did their level best to ignore our escalating spat about this Steve fellow.

"He lives downtown, on Worth Street. In Tribeca. You know his name—just look it up. It's easy. *Fook's sake.*"

Turning to go to the other end of the bar, Tony rejected me with his broad back. I quickly zeroed in on the *Ms*. There it was: his name and address and phone number. Ma Bell came through.

"Okay, great. Thanks."

As I scribbled the info on a bar napkin, Tony returned and leaned over the bar to close in on my face, eye to eye. We replayed a scene from years before, with my face in his hands.

"Damn it, Marcia.... You don't think I know, but I *do*. I warned you before, and I'm warning you now. I *know* what he is. I *know* what he's done. I *know* about the other woman and what he did to her. You don't know how I...*we all*...prayed that you would be okay...week after week. The guy is a goddamn *monster*."

Stunned, I looked up at Tony. What other woman? Steve was faithful, in his own peculiar way.

"Wait a minute.... What are you *talking* about? He was my boyfriend. There was no other woman...."

"I'm not talking about *dating* another woman. I'm not talking about a *girl*friend. I'm talking about *raping* a woman. He raped her at fookin' gunpoint. That's why he went to jail. You didn't *know* that?"

Rape. How could I have not known what the entire bar knew? I'd kept my bargain with his mother; I'd stayed silent and said nothing. And I'd never even *asked*.

"No."

"*Jay*sus."

The tears came quietly. Tony sighed the deepest of defeated sighs and walked back to the other end of the bar. I stared at my club soda and began my private negotiations. It's true he had done things, now I saw, *terrible* things, but never to *me*. It's true that he went to jail, but those were the *good* times. It's true that I should walk out and drop the whole idea, but…I wanted someone or something to stop what was rising up in me again. Erupting like sunspots around the black edges of my mind was a sadness that could kick an ibex off the Alps. I needed someone *familiar* to stabilize me just a little. Something I couldn't do for myself.

Thoughts of my father flew across my mind for a few seconds. He never hit *me*. And after all, it wasn't *so* bad, what he had done to me all those years ago. I just sat on his lap; simple. It really didn't *hurt* at all. The classically abused child, now an adult, sat up straight and negotiated it all away.

Steve never did *it* to *me*.

Yes. Sitting at the bar, I blew my nose with a bar napkin and concluded that on balance, Steve was the best option. I would go back to him.

Crumpling up the napkin, I shoved it into my coat pocket, threw a ten on the bar, and turned to walk out.

"Jaysus, *Marcia!*"

I heard his call as I pushed the restaurant door open to leave. The cackles from the bar patrons hit my ears; people who, I imagined, were "in the know," laughing, guffawing, even. Maybe they would rant on and on about what a sad sack of *shite* I was. The oboe player was brilliant, but she was a subnorm when it came to men. When the door slammed shut, I stayed next to it and listened with my ear leaned into the crack of the door.

"She's hopeless, Tony. Why even try?"

"I tell you, she's damaged. I can feel it in my guts. That girl's not fit to be with a man, any man. Especially *that* man."

"Okay, maybe that's true. That's all fine. But she's not your responsibility. Jesus, Tony, just let it go."

"You're right. I should, but I can't. I don't know why.... She's just so sad. She's got the biggest set of blinders on I've ever seen. She's always been odd and different, and she needs protecting."

"Yeah, good luck with *that*. You love her; *that's* your problem."

Tony paused, and I leaned in even closer.

"I do. Yeah, you're right: I *do* love her.... But not in that way. It's just that she can't love herself. And then she goes off with this goddamn mongrel of a man. And then a few years *later* she comes back for *more?* My God, I could commit *murder* when I think of him. With her."

"Okay, okay. Calm down. You'll probably never see her again. Tony, hit me again. Dewar's, on the rocks."

Softly I turned and walked away. My steps synced with the blood-red screaming shame that pulsed inside my every vessel. I was odd and different, Tony said. All my secrets were blasting out from my own megaphone for the entire world to muse about and discuss. I was like a small child who covers her eyes with her hands and assumes that because *she* can't see anything, the entire world can't see her. I didn't want to be weird. I wanted to be private and invisible. And blind.

Beginning my slow cadence, I headed downtown toward Tribeca. It was spring, and crowds of tourists were out and about, enjoying a perfect May evening in the Village. The street energy infused me with some momentum, and I began to feel rhythmically compact, my feet making a regular beat as I wound my way south toward Worth Street.

And as I walked with my inevitable and evenly paced gait, I resurrected the first fifteen bars of the "Liebestod" in my head. Longing, then desire. That half-diminished seventh chord. Unresolved, never ending. Tristan and Isolde, loving each other until death. But wasn't love supposed to be hopeful? Wasn't that what Isolde sang about, even as she was about to die?

I tromped down Sixth Avenue, then headed west over to Seventh, then south again. Crossing Houston Street, on to the other side of Canal, into Tribeca. Like a subservient Nazi in a goose step, I marched on and thought about the clever ways I'd lure Steve back and all the crafty tricks I'd use to force him to quit drinking, because I assumed that he was still drinking. My high steps, the perfect tempo for Isolde to sing her love song to Tristan, remained steady and comforted me. People walking toward me, against my path, fanned out and made room for my musical wake. *They* knew to get out of my way; the beautifully droning music in my head buffered me from all collisions, both physical and psychic.

Eleven Worth Street in Tribeca was the address, one of the first artists' cooperatives purchased by owner-tenants. You had to be working actively in your artistic profession in order to qualify to buy into the building. Based on his considerable glassblowing reputation, Steve had apparently made the cut. I stood in front of the building for a while, looking up, considering my next move. Dusk was approaching, and lights began to go on inside the apartments.

A phone booth stood on the corner of the street. I headed for it, dime prepared in my palm, fingers secured around it. Safely inside, with the doors pulled closed, I dug the crumpled napkin out of my pocket, slipped the dime in the slot, and made the call. My legs, having had a workout from their march southward, started to cramp as the ringing continued, and my scalp was running with sweat; the drips tickled around my damp collar. I badly needed to pee.

"Steve here."

Slamming the phone down, I laid my head against the filthy glass inside the phone booth, feeling like Mia Farrow, nine months pregnant in *Rosemary's Baby*, when she phones Charles Grodin, the "good" doctor. A recalibration of my nerves was in order, and I felt the need to review my mental checklist of why I was standing in a filthy phone booth on Worth Street making a call to someone Tony had called a mongrel, a monster, an animal. A rapist.

One more time. A fresh dime slid in.

"Yes."

His voice had the same intonation but just a bit of impatience now. I could hear him defiantly spit a fleck of tobacco from his tongue. That did it.

"Steve. It's me. I'm downstairs."

I waited about fifteen seconds and heard him drag on the Camel and then blow it out slowly, through pursed lips.

"Come up, Woo-Woo. Fourth floor."

It was that easy, his endearment for me: Woo-Woo. Sprinting across the street toward the building, I saw a fourth-floor light go on. The elevator opened to the loft space, and there stood my old Don Giovanni. A bit older, a lot grayer, and smiling a smile I never wanted to end: all for me. The villain glass eater took the skinny oboe player into his arms, and he smelled so damned normal, like a freshly washed Undy. Not a hint of licorice on him.

I took him in and was sweetly encouraged by his surroundings. The loft appeared surprisingly neat and tidy, with a decently furnished living area, a spare but functional kitchen along one wall, and a sleeping area at the back of the building. Warhols littered the walls, and I remembered he knew Andy. One Miró, surely from the family town house. A Klee propped in a corner. I had been prepared to see empty liquor bottles and a space overflowing with trash cans, a typical habitat for the drunkard I'd left a few years before.

While our arms were still entwined around each other, a small cat crept up and jumped onto Steve's shoulders and nestled down like a mink collar at the back of his head.

"Woo-Woo, meet Mousetrap."

Steve was purely, sweetly, and wholly domesticated. Freshly washed clothes, a decent home, sweet cigarette breath, and even a pet! Within the first ten minutes I recalibrated my lists and concluded that this *could* finally work. Wagner's murky halfdiminished chords turned into the hopeful chord progression of the Munchkins' song:

You're out of the woods.
You're out of the dark.
You're out of the night.
Step into the sun.
Step into the light…

We hugged and talked softly for a while as the shock of seeing each other began to wear off. We knew to dodge all the difficult stuff. Mousetrap stayed perched on his owner's neck, occasionally digging his claws in to keep balance as Steve shifted his weight. They had a nice symbiosis going. Mousetrap observed us both with soft cat eyes. And I kept my childlike hands over my eyes, making sure to see no evil.

We were hungry, and it was time to go out for a bite to eat. My insides seized. The ancient worries about his drinking roared back, with memories of trying to drag him out of bars before he got too badly off. As we walked toward the door, Mousetrap remained on his throne, behind Steve's head.

"Aren't you going to let him down?"

"Nope. Mousetrap goes with me everywhere."

"But won't he run away without a leash? He doesn't even have a *collar*."

"All I can say is his devotion to me is total and complete. Don't worry, Woo-Woo. Don't worry so much."

He winked at me as the three of us took the elevator down.

Once on the street, people passed by, smiling at our odd trio.

"Hi, Steve. Hi, Mousetrap."

The neighborhood was tight-knit. Who wouldn't know the guy with a cat wrapped around his neck? Mousetrap stayed glued to his collar all evening as we caught up, eating pasta and sipping club sodas. Ouzo didn't make an appearance. Not even a beer for a curtain call.

Steve was solidly impotent. All his years of hard-driven drinking and a three-pack-a-day cigarette habit had worked against his vascular system. His penis hung there, valiantly trying but ultimately shriveled, and we ended that first evening drifting off to sleep in a spoon position with Mousetrap above our heads on the pillow like a crown.

What a bonus: a penisless man for a boyfriend. A eunuch. I could take whatever he dished out (and I was still holding my breath), but I'd been released from doing hard time: sex. The pounding inevitability of what men wanted from me, beginning with my father, evaporated. After a few silly, frustrating, and laughable attempts, we let it go and just left it unspoken. Steve was my newly neutered Don G.

A tightly compartmentalized relationship quickly fell into place. We saw each other a few times a week in his area of town, with Mousetrap in tow. I was in the master's program, still supporting myself as a waitress and keeping a steely vise grip on my progress with the oboe; he was back to blowing glass in earnest. Our puzzle pieces seemed to fit.

Steve knew my drive to make art and had always given me a wide berth around music. Each of us worked hard in tandem during the day, and at night we became soft Grandma and Grandpa, devoted to their cat. We were quite a sight in Tribeca.

Occasionally on the weekends, I traveled out to his studio in Queens, not so far from the old Q100 bus, and watched while he blew. Metals mixed with glass, and the heat worked its wonderful alchemical magic of turning solid to liquid and then back to solid. The process of blowing was like ballet: Steve held the wand in the furnace, then pulled it out, turned it over, then into the glory hole, reshaping it all as the heating and cooling allowed the glass to reveal its own slithery intention. He couldn't stop until it was finished and he was satisfied with the shape and how all the metallic elements were settling inside the piece. The form then sat in the annealer for a day. The following day, he would examine his work and smash the rejects.

"Go ahead. Throw it in the barrel."

I was about to destroy works of art, with his blessing.

"Really? Are you sure? What's wrong with it?"

"Well, I'm not happy with how the two metals merged in these pieces....I have to figure out a way to keep them separate inside the piece so that they don't combine into a new color. My timing was off. It's all about heat and control once I insert the metals into the glass."

"But are you *sure?*"

"Just think of it as a bad reed. And don't worry, Woo-Woo. Don't worry so much."

"Okay, if you say so! Here goes!"

Smash! Into the barrel went a dozen pieces from the day before. Those that were spared were placed on a long, carefully lit shelf to be evaluated over a period of days and weeks. Then the final selection went out for sale or exhibition. Very few made that cut. It *was* similar to reed making: you had to be willing to destroy with no sentiment and start over.

Don't worry, Woo-Woo. Emasculating a man with a gun-penis complex by smashing his artwork, even with his benign encouragement. Who did I think I was? *Woo-Woo. You worry too much.*

I walked into the loft one late afternoon, wary because I had not heard from him for a few days. Steve didn't have an answering machine, but I knew when he usually hit the loft after spending a day at the studio.

It was quiet. Mousetrap trotted toward me, slinking in between and around my legs as I approached the kitchen. His food and water bowls were empty, so I refilled them, and he settled in to his meal. I heard movement, Steve in the back of the loft behind the screen that separated the living space from the bed area. I could see his silhouette as he rose from the bed and began to languidly pace.

"Woo-Woo. C'mere."

"Steve, what's happening? Mousetrap was starving."

"Forget Mousetrap. He's fine. Just c'mere."

I turned into the bed area. Red-faced, drunk, smelling of licorice, he stood before me, using his hand to get steady at the brick wall by the head of the bed. Three guns lay neatly in a row on the bed.

"Steve, *what the hell?*"

Without a word, he roared forward with his arms extended ramrod straight, both hands formed into fists. He punched me hard in the chest with the full weight of his two hundred pounds. I skidded on the wood floor in a backwards, upside-down crab position. Scrambling to right myself, I crawled into a corner of the room and instinctively put my feet up.

"Steve, *please.* Don't."

"Please what? Don't what?"

"Please. Just leave me alone."

"I can't."

"Why not?"

"Because I just can't."

Mousetrap began crying in another area of the loft.

Don G. loomed over me, hands balled up. He was drunk and steady, breathing in and out through his nose, his lips curled around his teeth and sucked into his mouth, as he looked at me with a calm hatred that was inexplicable, because I knew I didn't deserve it. I'd never seen this particular combination of facial expressions before, and I was momentarily confused more than anything. Maybe this is what the woman of the "hurt" had seen in his eyes. With my legs still in the air, ready for his next attack, I negotiated with him to let me go.

"Steve, I just want to leave."

"You can't."

"But *why?*"

"You just can't."

"What did I do?"

"Don't you know?"

"No. Just *tell* me, and I'll fix it."

"You can't fix it."

"Then let me leave, and we can talk about it tomorrow."

"You can't leave."

"Why not?"

"Don't you know?"

"No. I don't get it."

"You don't *have* to get it. There's nothing to get."

"But—"

"Woo-Woo? Shut the fuck up."

He came at me with both fists at the end of his arms, again double-barreled. I thrust my feet into his body, throwing him back onto the bed. Guns skittered off and rattled to the floor. He quickly reached for one of them.

Instantly I realized he wasn't that drunk; his stretch for the gun was much too swift for a truly drunk man. Scrambling to my feet, I raced for the door, taking the stairs down the four flights to the street.

I slammed myself into the same corner phone booth I'd used four months before. Panting and feeling sick to my stomach, I sank to the filthy floor, my legs instinctively bracing against the louvered door. My chest, my sternum, began to ache so badly I thought I might be having a heart attack.

After a few more minutes, I got my breathing under control and looked down at the source of the ache. He'd hit me hard with a double-fisted sucker punch right above the breasts. A quarter-size circle of blood oozed through my blouse just over my right breast and was spreading fast. Curious, I looked down, under my shirt. There, in my skin, was the imprint of a penguin; I had been impaled by its beak.

Steve collected penguins in all forms: glass penguins, of course; ceramic penguins; wooden penguins. While he was in Rikers, I'd hired a metalsmith to make a ring with a small solid-silver penguin mounted on the band and presented it to him the day he was released. He wore this ring on his left ring finger. My gift had been turned on me.

Over the next hour, I sat as if in a passive vigil—unable to move, watching the building. Only one person approached the booth to make a call. He tried to open the door unsuccessfully, as my legs stiffened against his attempts. Eventually he looked down at the floor of the booth, only to see a girl looking back up, bleeding from her heart, motionless. Our eyes met. He blinked and walked away.

Night fell; the booth began to fog up from my breath. For the first time in a very long time, I could not summon up music. I was bone dry.

In the weeks that followed, the wound became infected and simply wouldn't heal. The stab had been deep, gouging into my flesh. Some form of dangerous bacteria must have been living on the beak tip, and it was as if he wanted me to never forget him and what he could do. He got his wish. That inner wound. *My* wound. Nothing ever seemed to heal.

Danny

A master's degree nearly in hand, you've practiced like crazy, for hours and hours, making hundreds and hundreds of reeds. People seem to be impressed with your playing, resulting in some well-paying New York City freelance jobs. You gradually rebalance the way you make your living: less waitressing and more concerts. The complete turnaround does not take long.

There's a brilliant player in town named Danny, whom you approach for lessons. He's several years older and plays in some very established groups. You love his musicianship, which impresses you as brave and impeccable. He agrees to teach you. You go in for the first lesson with the Strauss Oboe Concerto. You play the first page. He works on it with you and gives you some suggestions. A month later you go back for the next lesson and continue with the Strauss concerto. At the end of the lesson, he asks you if you have ever worked on the Gillet Études. You admit you have not. The Gillet Études focus on one aspect of technical difficulty per étude. One may deal with trills. One will address arpeggios. One will cover all the major and minor scales. Danny recommends that you buy the set and bring in Étude number 1 for the next lesson. You purchase the Gillet Études, and you dis-

cover that the first étude is extremely difficult. You can't play it at all.

But you practice very hard and go in for the next lesson. After you fumble around on it, he reaches over, grabs your oboe, and plays through the étude, on your oboe and your reed, without stopping. Perfectly. He hands your oboe back and says, "Okay, let's go. Start with the first line." You begin to play and then start to cry. "C'mon," he says. "I know the good stuff comes after the tears. I know women. Let's go. Again."

You play and cry. He makes you continue, even though you're blubbering through the reed and the music. You want to run out of his apartment. You feel like a fraud. Who cares about your stupid sound? So what if it's beautiful? You can't play the fucking oboe.

Over the next year and a half you study the first twelve études of Gillet with Danny. You fall in love with him and then out of love with him. He never knows about the love part. After a year and a half, you can play Gillet number 1 through number 12 perfectly. Now, Danny says, you can call yourself an oboist. You start over on the Strauss concerto.

Burt

MY MUSIC CAREER had kicked up dust nicely, and I enjoyed an added glow to my work as I began to receive invitations to play high-profile concerts with well-known musicians. Dancing between these disparate venues—being a freelance orchestral player one week and a soloist out in front of an orchestra the next—was a commonplace juggling act for me, much like shifting gears when playing Bach and Stravinsky on the same program.

Racing out the door one day, I grabbed the phone as it rang. Somewhat harried after packing up quickly, I was late, and I hated to be late for any rehearsal.

"Is Marcia there?"

"This is Marcia."

"Marcia, this is André Watts calling."

"André?"

"André Watts...the pianist."

"Um, hi!"

I dropped my gig bag on the table and sat down with a thump.

"How are you?"

"Ah...fine, I guess."

"Well, the reason I'm calling is I'm putting together a chamber music tour of the United States for next season, and I wondered whether you would be available to join us."

"Wow. *Sure.*"

Now I was *sure* to be late. But I had the excuse of a lifetime.

"Great. Well, let me explain a bit more. I'm programming some wind and piano music. I've always noticed and loved your playing when I've heard you within the orchestra on concerto dates. Your sound is quite extraordinary. You seem to be a very engaged player—I tend to notice such things through the years, as you might imagine."

I supposed I *could* imagine this. André was an icon, a giant in the business. He'd performed with virtually every conceivable orchestra throughout his long career. Not to mention sandwiching in Carnegie Hall solo recital dates, year after year.

"Thank you so much. I'm a bit in shock, I guess."

"Well, don't be. Or at least try *not* to be. I don't bite."

We both laughed and managed to pull the tension out of the exchange.

"No. No, of course not! André, I'm thrilled. Just tell me the dates, and I'll be there."

The tour was booked—about ten concerts throughout the United States. During the year leading up to the tour—because such things are scheduled at least one year in advance—André and I got to know each other, enjoying a few leisurely dinners when he was in town. When he was out on the road during that interim time, he called now and then and our acquaintanceship gradually turned into a comfortable camaraderie, almost friendship. Having committed to performing with me, André needed to know the human being behind the instrument, especially with a touring engagement in the offing.

I had long since stopped asking or even hoping my parents would attend my concerts. But André and the halo of his superstardom beckoned, which proved the tipping point for my parents. Suddenly, overnight, I was *worth* listening to. I became legitimate, soaring above the cream of Katie Gibbs graduates. We were scheduled to perform at the Toledo Museum of Art—in the hometown of *Margery Bloor Wenner: Brains and Beauty.* They booked their plane tickets to Ohio.

André was a generous and intense colleague onstage. Just before we walked out to perform the Poulenc Oboe Sonata, he would take a quick inhalation and exhalation of breath, then nod to me. For those fifteen minutes, as we performed together, the audience and even the world seemed to fall away, and we were as connected as any two human beings might be. With concentration and attunement so compacted, I imagined the pores on my skin opening to accept whatever came, second after second after second.

Throughout the weekend in Toledo, between social obligations with our relatives and the concert itself, Wotan kept a clear distance from both André and me. He watched me on the stage, vulnerable, at large, yet in my private world. Remaining apart and at the perimeter of the action, he stood with a competitive edge. I'd turn my head, and there his eyes were, like the *Mona Lisa's*, trained on me, following me everywhere. I'd dressed in a sleeveless, form-fitting concert gown—perhaps not the best choice of garment. I began to feel sheepish and undeserving, all brought on by my father's crushing glances. My old negotiating partner was sullying my moment in the sun.

After the concert, in casual conversation, he mentioned that he and my mother would be hosting a large Thanksgiving dinner in New Hampshire, where they had recently retired.

"Oh, great," I said instinctively. "I'll come up, too. I'd love to come."

"No—don't come. The house will be too crowded."

"Okay. But I can stay in a motel close by. I don't need to stay in the house."

"No. It's too many people."

"But I'll only come for the main meal, then. Would that help?"

"I said no. It's just better if you stay home."

The cruelty of the moment kicked me down, and I became rigid, imagining myself sitting on his lap, not wanting to move a fraction of an inch for fear of what I would surely feel; in front of the TV on a Sunday night, while listening to Andy Williams sing "Moon River" on *The Ed Sullivan Show*.

My father turned around and walked the length of the large reception room—my eyes now on his broad back. I placed a small chunk of cheddar cheese from the banquet table in my mouth, chewed slowly, washed it down with a swig of white wine, and thought of Burt Lancaster and Deborah Kerr rolling around in the surf in the movie *From Here to Eternity*. This was a 1950s version of a sex scene—their affair is spoken about, though we never see them do more than kiss. But the sexual nature of them, entangled in the water as it ebbed and flowed like an orgasm, is clear. I watched that movie many times over the years, and Burt's back, as he lolled in the surf with Deborah, was particularly intriguing to me. I waited for that scene every time.

One night when I was perhaps nine or ten, I walked out of my room to go to the bathroom and saw my father standing at the end of the hall with his back to me, naked. His back had the exact same cut as Burt Lancaster's—broad up top and tapering through the torso down to the waist. He heard me and turned, revealing his full nakedness. I was startled, but he remained calm and made no effort to cover up, which at the time was particularly scary and horrifying. My eyes dropped down for just a second, to take in what I saw as three penises—or three long droopy things. Then my eyes quickly shot back up to his. Holding my gaze, he walked toward me and placed his hands on my shoulders (in exactly the way he'd put his hands on my shoulders when he'd asked if I was "comfortable"). Swiveling me around and with his hand at the small of my back, he nudged me forward. I went into the bathroom, alone, and closed the door.

Once inside, I sat on the toilet, hyperventilating. My father as a sexual being, a man who was not embarrassed to show his special daughter of nine years his naked body, felt wrong and violating. Why didn't he make an effort to cover up? His casual manner was evidence of his perceived and actual power over me. He had absolutely nothing to be sorry about or, in fact, hide, and further, I was not important enough to make him exhibit even a pretense of modesty. I hadn't thought about that event, or the connection to my interest in Burt Lancaster's body, until I saw my father's back after the concert.

As audience members milled about, I began to crumble in slow motion. André stood just a few feet away, speaking with friends. A few concertgoers approached to compliment my playing. I thanked them in what must have been a monotone. Time moved forward as if all were normal, but the blood beat hard from my heart directly to my head. Childlike and flummoxed, I sought my father's eyes, *my* eyes asking what on earth I had done wrong. He'd left the room.

Repeats

For the American premiere of the Philip Glass opera White Raven *at Lincoln Center in 2001, you receive the call and agree to play the run. You love Glass's music specifically for how it reminds you, strangely, personally, of Wagner. The harmonic changes are extremely slow, and you can wallow in E minor, for instance, for thirty minutes or even longer. Wagner is like that. You love that languorous, ocean liner–like movement in music. As you stare at the boat, it appears to be anchored, but after a while, you notice that your eyes are at a different point on the horizon. You love to feel stable within music's velvety language.*

You remember seeing Einstein on the Beach *at Brooklyn Academy of Music in 1984. It was Glass's breakout opera. You remember thinking that it was like seeing Stanley Kubrick's* 2001: A Space Odyssey *for the first time. You didn't understand it, but you couldn't rip your eyes away. While watching* Einstein, *you were mesmerized by the slow-moving "action" on the stage, juxtaposed with the rapid repeating patterns in the orchestra, laid over huge swaths of static, harmonic landscapes. A few other composers had written "minimal" music like this, but no one had merged it with a dramatic, staged concept. You could say that Robert Wilson, who staged the opera, was a perfect fit for Glass's musical vocabulary. Fast repeating chords and arpeggios set against the giant man on stilts lumbering across the stage for ten minutes. Each man's art becomes stronger when linked together.*

With this new score on your stand, you see immediately that Glass's music will be particularly challenging because of its repeating patterns for many dozens of bars. The notes themselves are not that hard to play. It's the repetition that's mind-numbingly tricky, because you can get mixed up easily. You have to be very alert and on your game. In addition to the repeated patterns of notes to play, the small sections are also repeated and then large sections, too. Then there could be a huge repeat, when you go back and do the whole thing over again. Without ever stopping. These sections can last for ten to fifteen minutes. That is a very long time when you are playing repeated patterns. The whole thing keeps folding over onto itself, and because the harmony is so static, you don't know where you are sometimes. And because the chords are basically simple and don't change much, if you make a mistake with the repeat, it is very obvious. There is nowhere to hide in Mr. Glass's music. It is extremely exposed, even though many musicians are playing the same exact notes.

So you realize that this opera is one of the hardest things you have ever played. But you are in luck, because the man with the eyes and ears and nose and arms is your conductor for the run. Not only does he have the phenomenally gifted physicality to get the job done, he also has the genius ability to keep track of all the repeats and all the stuff on the stage. God. What a brain!

And when people do mess up their repeats, he just smiles. You want to play perfectly for him, because he is such a gentleman about the mistakes!

Gradually, through the rehearsals, everyone pulls his or her act and mind together, and it's super tight for the run of the performances. But the Glass opera makes you start to think about how the whole world is one enormous repeat; that there is nothing new at all. And you begin to develop a fascination with fractals and perfect proportions and certain colors like red and the golden mean and even the universal elements of the solar system that seem to hold the whole earth up and simultaneously keep it spinning. And repeating feels fundamental and natural and a God-given right. You have done your own fair share of repeating.

Florida

AFTER THE TOUR of my lifetime, André receded quickly back into his own life, shy an oboe player. That made sense. My parents retreated to New Hampshire and resumed their retired life, hosting all manner of people for Thanksgiving, minus an oboe player. For that, I had been well prepared.

The memory of my father's broad back turning on me sent me skirting the rim of a 23rd Street sewer. At that exact moment I needed a yes-man: one who would shepherd me to the sidewalk, away from the open manhole, and reverse the very direction of the drain's orbit-driven vortex. I would now repeat *myself*; nab a tried-and-true yes-man whose worst habits were already well known to me. The devil himself would do.

My broken-in Mephisto was now living in a warm climate—halfway to hell: the west coast of Florida, on a barrier island called Anna Maria Island. Gone were the horns. His spear, chucked aside. His blood-red devil skin had been nicely neutralized by a tropical tan.

As I approached Bruce's lean, lanky figure from the arrivals gate at the airport, I saw a bronzed Clint with the whitest set of choppers imaginable. Those teeth glared and blared! Well, you've got to be unnaturally tanned and have teeth bonded with pure white enamel that God didn't invent if you mean to do right by the state of Florida.

Our reunion had been conceived of and arranged with expeditious fluidity a month prior. It was simple: I'd called and left a message on his answering machine. Within four days, I received a note in the post, with a poem.

Bruce was a literary man of deep talents and accomplishments. In addition to writing copy for big advertising agencies, he was a published poet, with two mildly bestselling books in the 1970s Rod McKuen style of romantic poetry. He drew very well and had sold a few cartoons in his day. Photography was the most brilliant aspect of his oeuvre, with a special nod toward the female face, shot through gauze and tightly focused through the aperture of his beloved Hasselblad camera.

The poem hit the right notes. It seemed that I made someone weak; I caused someone to dream; I inspired someone to need me. I was likened to the wonders of nature. I booked a flight for All Points South.

The vestiges of our brutal marriage still lived close to the surface of my skin, and, careful and restrained, I maintained a hesitantly optimistic skepticism during our first weekend together. We talked, and Bruce was a *great* talker. But the bulk of his bluster had been punched out of him. With the severance package from his European days assiduously blown through, he was subsisting on freelance copywriting jobs and the occasional photography shoot. The freshly humbled devil now lived a very spare life.

Professing his remorse repeatedly for messing up my life, Bruce now allowed me to assume what was for me, certainly in light of our previous relationship, an unusual position of power. I enjoyed being apologized to, so I sat back on the sofa and let it all flow from him like a roaring, whitecapped river. His mea culpas were stated, rethought, and rephrased on the fly. Bruce more than proved his competence as a clever copywriter. He pressed his point, and his love, well.

Once home, I received a letter each and every day. As a scribe, Bruce was the sweetest, most understanding of lovers. Self-deprecation seemed a newfound trait, and to highlight his new lowly status all the more, he steadily raised my pedestal higher, draping it with garlands of adulation concerning my accomplished career as an oboist. On paper: our love was big and pure and tremulous. In hell: paper disappears with the flick of a match.

The poem he wrote to me, which propelled me to Florida, eventually found its way into my wallet. While in rehearsal, or even on the subway, I often pulled it out for a cursory read-through, as if to emboss the beauty of his words more deeply into my doubtful mind. Like a blind person, I'd run my fingers over the type-punched indentations of the B side. His words sprang into a three-dimensional reality, and I rubbed my cheek up close to the paper and his idea of who I was.

This poem. Its words reminded me that someone saw me in a way I couldn't possibly see myself; that someone thought I was beautiful and worth aching over. Those words made *me* ache. Even in years past, when he was addled by drugs and alcohol, Bruce's most desperate compulsion was a need for passion, and I'd always found that attractive. Now this poem was proof that a fevered passion could still bubble up, with me as his muse. It had been summoned up as a response to—no, as a *tribute* to—a single voice message left on his answering machine.

By the time I went down for the second trip, all my worries went up in smoke—gone. I believed this poem to be pure and purely inspired:

I am lost,
As I surrender myself to you
In this silent pursuit
Of shared pleasures.
Your naked perfection has
Swept me away, away
To the absolute center
Of my tiny universe,
That invisible focus of
All my most gentle fantasies.

Modernism called to this newly bronzed wordsmith—his small condo was all glass, mirrors, and white laminate. During our second weekend together, I noticed lovely touches like purple irises on the marble Saarinen table in the dining area. Bed linens were freshly laundered, *ironed,* and pulled down as they would be in a luxury hotel. The white-and-black bathroom was pristine and smelled faintly of lavender. How nice that he'd thought to impress me. Bruce, now clean and sober, was truly a romantic.

It was evening on the second night; we were preparing to step out for dinner. Having come in from a day at the beach, we'd lazed off to sleep for an hour. Now Bruce was in the bathroom, showering. A long, low bookshelf was mounted on the wall opposite his bed, floating about twenty inches off the floor. Lying on my side, waiting for my turn under the sand-blasting shower,

I lazily perused his books with mild curiosity. Bruce read a lot, mostly the classics. I saw *Moby-Dick,* a few Jane Austens, some Elmore Leonard—Philip Roth, of course.

My eyes stopped short at several copies of both volumes of his poetry. I couldn't help but muse back to the day I had moved out on him. His mouth foaming with spittle, he had charged me several times, and my boys from the bar literally stood in between us and faced him down.

The last thing Bruce and I had fought about was his poetry.

"Aren't you going to take the books?" was one of his parting shots.

The volumes he'd given me early in our relationship were stacked on top of the coffee table. Of course they were signed copies, and I actually *wanted* to take them. But his pathetic narcissism ran roughshod over any sentiment that remained. I screamed the last laugh as I walked out the door.

"Fuck your stupid, vapid poetry. Are you serious with that drivel anyway? It's complete and utter *shit!*"

Victorious, the door slammed shut, and I tromped down the stairs with Spot in tow.

Now here I was in Florida, wooed by that very same vapid (now revered) shit. And quite possibly staring at my very own signed copies of said revered shit. A confusing surge of adrenaline kicked up. I didn't want to look at them, afraid of a visceral reaction I might experience if I saw the inscriptions he wrote those years before, words fueled by artifice and evil.

Bruce continued his shower. My hand dropped down to the spines of the books, my fingers gently brushing the jackets. They looked new, not dog-eared at all. Maybe he kept new copies on hand to woo potential Florida girlfriends. Poetry was certain to seal the deal. I felt my cynicism crank up a notch.

Shoving all suspicious thoughts aside, I pulled out one of the volumes. It was not my signed copy. My mind temporarily eased, and, letting out a stream of air, I started to flip through the pages. My thumb happened to stop on a page where I landed on the words:

I am lost,
As I surrender myself to you
In this silent pursuit
Of shared pleasures.

My poem.

Bruce was a first-class, self-plagiarizing, lazy-eyed devil! That piece of paper I'd lugged around and nurtured and caressed for weeks—a fraud on a massive scale, just a bunch of words strung together years ago off the backside of another, younger woman's body.

The flow of the shower stopped, and Bruce was whistling as he toweled off in the bath. He did that a lot—whistling—and suddenly I found it irritating. I quickly jumped up and began stacking all the books that were in the bookcase on the bed, assembling my arsenal.

He stepped out of the bathroom, wrapped in a towel. The light from above the sink cut him in half: deeply tanned upper torso, bright white towel below. It was hard to discern his facial expression. He may have been smiling or looking bewildered when he saw the stacked books on the bed. I'll never know.

The onslaught began. I aimed at his head, where that poem,

written for someone else, had been birthed. I aimed to smash his brains in, with book after book, and give him black eyes and a broken nose to mar his Clint Eastwood looks. I aimed to chip his gleaming row of front teeth but good.

"Marcia! *Fuck!* What's the matter? Jesus. Stop it!"

His arms raised in a protective stance, trying to bat off the flurry of *American Pastoral* and *Pride and Prejudice.*

"My POEM. My *fucking poem!*"

As he looked down at the top of the bookshelf, in two seconds his eyes clicked. My yes-man was very smart. He saw the book and *knew.* Only a person with malice in his original intent could discern the problem so immediately.

Bruce collapsed on the bed and seemed to settle in for what he knew he deserved. His nose oozed blood, and with each whack of a book the blood spattered onto his pristine white bed-cover. I wanted to do better: I wanted to destroy him.

Bruce and Steve, my mother, my father. I wanted to kill every person in my life who had, openly or with secrecy, face-to-face or from a pummeling distance, killed an oboist's soul. I wanted to destroy all the yes-people who were my unwitting partners against myself.

But I stopped. *I* was not a killer of person or soul.

"Marcia, *Jesus!* I think you broke one of my ribs."

"Good."

"I'm serious! I can't *breathe.* I have stabbing pains in my chest."

"*Good.* Whether it's a heart attack or a broken rib, I'm *glad.* Because I want you to *suffer!* You *fucker.*"

"I'm sorry."

"Good."

"No, I'm *really* sorry."

"I believe *ZERO* of what you say. You're spewing shit. One hundred percent."

"When I sent the poem, I didn't know if we were even going to get together!"

"I read that goddamned poem *every day*. And it's a *fucking fraud*."

"That's not true. It really does mean what I feel about you. But how would I know that you'd get all attached to it?"

Ah, the mitigating. The buts and all the many other reasons…

"It doesn't matter. *All* that. It's still just shit. You're a has-been. An enormous recycling bin. Worse! You fucking *trash heap!*"

His breathing was shallow and rapid. Too bad. He probably needed a doctor. So what? I wasn't ready to relieve his physical agony, because I loved watching him squirm. Watching a man suffer—any man—might do the trick for me. Bruce was just in my firing line, one step in front of a string of men in my life.

"Tell me why you're sorry."

"Okay. Um…it was wrong, and…I was lazy."

"Not good enough. Tell me what you're sorry about."

"I'm sorry I sent that poem. I should've sat down and written something new.…But I can't write like that anymore.…It's all kind of dried up.…"

"Excuses. Tell me why you're sorry."

He shrugged.

"All the stuff I just said…what else *is* there?"

I gave him a withering stare. "It's not about the fucking poem, and you *know* it."

Bruce took a long, slow breath, shuddering with the pain of his supposed broken rib.

"I know, I know....But can I have a glass of water? I'm parched."

"FUCK, NO! Tell me what you're sorry about. *Then* you can have a drink."

Taking another rasping breath, he seemed to deflate before my eyes.

"Okay. Okay."

He looked at me for several seconds and then closed his eyes.

"You were the most loving person I ever met. But I couldn't handle that. Or your talent. So I had to get you down to a level where I felt I was superior to you. I had to wipe you out and your oboe, too. I knew very well what I was doing—breaking you to pieces day after day. And I've regretted that since the day you left me. No one deserved it less, and no one could defend herself less. I'm very sorry for those years. I was a bastard....But I'm here *now*."

I kicked him in the foot; the tremors of pain traveled up to his chest. Opening his eyes, he winced with a shuddering intake of breath.

"Bruce, you always *were* a step below a Hallmark card."

His eyes widened with resigned recognition. Bruce had always been very quick to disparage other copywriters' work by characterizing it as "a step above Hallmark." Now he slowly let his head bang back onto the wall, accepting our secret little joke.

I sat still, taking in the violence and the words, trying to figure out which was worse.

"Now let me tell *you* what you should be sorry about. You just couldn't follow the fucking rules. And my rules were very simple. I will put up with just about anything. Happy to do it. Happy to oblige. But what I expect is that *any* man leaves my oboe the hell alone. That's always been my line in the sand. And you come along with your drugs and your ego and your incessant ranting about your stupid former life in Europe and your ridiculous career that was all shot to shit. But you just couldn't let me have that one thing. The one thing that was separate from you. And you got me to a state where I went along with you, and I almost lost it *all*. All my other men, *without exception,* let me have my oboe. *All my men.* Including my father. That was the rule. That was the bargain. That was the *agreement.*"

He looked at me with newly interested eyes.

"What in the hell does your *father* have to do with this? Marcia? Tell me what you *mean!*"

He was now screaming and managed to get up off the bed and approach me. I turned my back on him.

"My father. Okay?"

I whispered a truth that I'd never uttered. My chin dropped to my chest; I closed my eyes and felt the shame trying to push through my eyelids. I could hear his shallow breath close behind me. When I turned back to face him, our eyes exchanged a deadened look, filled with a new knowledge that couldn't be forgotten.

"Get it *now?*"

My tone was flippant, mocking.

"*Mother of God.* Marcia. My poor Marcia."

"Yeah, well, don't get all sentimental on me."

But I was starting to cry, feeling mildly regretful after my book-throwing attack. I nudged him in the foot as I went into the kitchen for his glass of water.

"Mother*fucker.*"

As he sipped his water, Bruce watched me, wary and sad. Tight-lipped, soundless, I wept.

Eventually I broached the subject of getting him some help.

The place was in shambles, but I managed to find his car keys and help him to his feet and into sweatpants, a T-shirt, and sandals. I used rough fingers, jostling him when I could under the pretext of helping him with my guiding hands.

The emergency room admitted him with one bruised rib. An eye slightly blackened; his dental work, just fine. Bruce earnestly explained to the doctors that he had been mugged, and the thugs, a bunch of young boys (ever the copywriter), ran off with some money.

My muscles remained sore for the next week, having found out firsthand what kind of physical strength it takes to hurt someone. I burned Bruce's poem, washing it down the drain to the sewers of hell.

A few months later I received a call from Bruce's sister. He had taken a gun to his mouth in a suicide attempt but survived. With half his face blown off, he was now a mute vegetable living in a VA hospital in Florida.

Was I responsible for this? He'd tried to explain himself, yet I was steadfast and harsh in my rejection of his apologies. I felt awful: cruel and cold. But underneath I held tight to a dry sense of detachment. The truth was, I was relieved that my secret about my father was once again a secret—still unknown to anyone but me.

Designated

For classical musicians, taking on commercial work, such as sub-bing on Broadway shows, is motivated by making money. It is one square on the patchwork quilt that defines a freelancer's musical life. But it is not beneath you. As a matter of fact, it's some of the most challenging work you do, because the requirements are specialized and exacting. Broadway musicians have a great contract: they can take off up to four shows in an eight-show week and still keep the gig. Most Broadway musicians will accept work outside the show. It helps them keep their playing fresh and gives them the opportunity to have variety in their musical experience. So substitutes are needed from time to time. That's when you get the call.

You want to make the big music. But when you play in a Broadway show, you have to nip all your big ideas in the bud. A Broadway show is run with the understanding that eight shows a week must look and sound exactly the same from day to day. The consistency of what an audience sees and hears is extremely important to the creative team. When you stand in for a regular player, your main goal is to play perfectly and sound as much like the regular player as possible. You do not want to be noticed.

To prepare for your first subbing experience, you first do something called "watching the book." You show up at the theater at about 7:30 p.m., enter the stage door, and go downstairs into the bowels of the theater: past all the dressing rooms in which the stars are readying, past the dressers preparing the costumes, past the chorines warming up, past the makeup rooms, past the stagehands playing poker while they wait for the curtain to go up. Finally, you get to the area where the musicians hang out, usually a table, some chairs, and a row of lockers, which is typically right by the door to the orchestra pit. The regular oboist, whom you'll be subbing for, greets you. Bringing a folding chair into the already jam-packed pit, you place it right next to his. Then you just go back to the musicians' area and chat until they call, "Places." "Places" means that the show is about to start.

You just sit there for the next two-plus hours and "watch the music" as he performs the show. Actually you know this oboist very well; you've played many concerts together through the years. You know his sound and listen carefully to the way he plays the show, for his specific musical inflections, because you'll try to imitate these when you actually go in for your first performance.

You watch the conductor and see what he's up to. The show may be very straightforward, or it might be extremely tricky, and how the conductor guides the orchestra is important to notice and remember. The show ends, you take a copy of the music home to practice, and two days later, you show up to play your first performance as a sub.

Subbing in a Broadway show the first time is particularly nerve-racking because you never actually have the opportunity to rehearse—you just go in and perform. It's an odd thing and not the normal way that musicians prepare for performances. Normally, you practice at home, you rehearse with the ensemble quite a lot, and then you perform. When you sub for the first time, you're just thrown to the wolves, sink or swim.

You want to play everything correctly. You don't want to sound too different. And most important, you don't want to step in the cracks—in other words, get a little lost during the show and end up playing in the wrong place. Then things sound strange, and the conductor looks down because he's startled. You never want the conductor to be startled and look at you. You want the conductor to not even know you are there.

When it's over, the conductor might have notes for you or he might not say a word. If he's silent, you lie awake all night, reliving the show, trying to figure out if you did a good enough job. Then you go in to sub for the second time. This is much harder. You have the false assumption that you actually know the show simply because you played it once, about a week ago. In fact, the second show is where people make the most mistakes.

After the second time around, the conductor decides whether he will "designate" you. If you are designated, it means that you can sub in an unlimited capacity for this show. If you are not, you can sub only on a limited basis.

If you are not designated you are demoralized, pummeled. You may fall into a deep depression for weeks. You question everything you do on the oboe. All because of the whim of a Broadway conductor. And by the way, he wasn't so hot at his job, either. Then the next week you happen to perform the Carter Oboe Concerto.

A Sister

THE LAST TIME I'd seen Jinx was years before, during an early morning drug deal at Palsson's. Once she'd recovered from the stint at Bellevue, she slipped back into her role in my life: the person Bruce and I could call in desperation, at the bottom of a 2:00 a.m. totem pole, when our regular connections didn't—or couldn't—answer the phone. The early morning hours tugged us to our knees, and we were more than happy to take her watered-down product. Still, we laughed about our deal of last resort. Cocaine makes both the lowly and the highfalutin feel good about their starting position in a fifty-yard dash. It doesn't really matter who is first off the block.

Jinx was a dead ringer for Michelle Pfeiffer: truly a drop-dead stunner. Heads swiveled wherever she went, and a late night at Palsson's was no different. That last evening, while Bruce and I itched at our drinks, waiting for her delivery, the door finally swung open, and she made her triumphal entrance—all necks craned to see the five-foot-ten goddess dressed in an outfit to beat back the natives, gloriously out of their league. She easily sashayed in four-inch heels. I felt dwarfed and mousy, jealous of her ability to draw an adoring crowd. Bellevue Hospital had receded like a distant tableau on an opera set.

Now, more than a decade later, I considered Jinx and what our different places in society looked like. My hard-earned reputation as a respected musician surely kept me well perched on rungs much higher than her towering stilettos. But we both swung low, rappelling off a granite cliff at the end of a big, thick, husky rope strung up by my father. He'd chiseled at us both, sculpting our two distinct versions of womanhood: Jinx at the receiving end of his curled knuckles, while his soft, splayed paws deftly, secretly, kneaded at me.

Bruce was as good as dead. I imagined his head alternately lolling and snapping back and forth, his face vivisected, ghastly in appearance. I was back in New York, sleeping long hours and ruminating on the high, the low, the beautiful, and the newly deformed. Rueful or jaded, maybe that's why I thought of my sister.

I sent Jinx a short note, wishing her well. She called immediately.

"Marcia? It's Jinx!"

Her high-pitched, hysterical manner of speech, always just a bit too loud and insistent—a bit too enthusiastic—jarred.

"I'm really glad you wrote! How are you?!"

"I'm fine. It's been a long time."

"I know!"

On it went, as we caught up over a lengthy first phone call. She played the wronged heroine to the hilt; surely a hard-fought role, perfected through her well-documented defiance of our father. I certainly remembered it all, and soft sympathy, perhaps even compassion, quickly welled up in me.

I couldn't reciprocate with my own counterpart of such a

tragic opera. To the world, and, most deeply, to myself, I was still tightly battened down about my abuse. With the exception of Bruce, no one *ever* knew about my shameful past with my father. Because I was choked up and stuffed down, my oboe was the only vulnerable voice the world would hear. And I would not perform a confessional quid pro quo with Jinx; I divulged only what was safe, what I felt she needed from me.

Jinx had a phobia about flying, so I agreed to travel to Miami Beach, where she lived. When we came face-to-face during that first weekend visit, her truly tragic past staggered me while her new sobriety struck me as monumentally impressive. We were sisters yet virtually strangers, filling in the gaping holes of the years of lives hard-lived.

Delighted with this newly attentive family member, I scheduled trips to see Jinx around my concert schedule and occasionally made the ultimate sacrifice: I turned down jobs to be with her. We were *blood*, bonding together, now like fired-up aluminum on steel. For many months I hid this sister act—Electra and Iphigenia—from my parents.

Jinx quickly became the tree trunk of my family. Indeed, this was the first time in my life that I was able to even imagine what a family relationship might resemble, much less actually live it. And I was hungry for it; voracious, really. I began to count on her for real emotional connection, and she reciprocated with an easy disclosure of the minutiae of her life, past and present-day. I felt honored that she thought so highly of me—to trust me with her story. And because I believed that she had had the harder time of it with my father, I wanted to do right by her in every way.

My naive desire was to be the best little sister imaginable. And as usual, with family and men alike, I put the horse blinders on and staggered blithely forward, jumping to conclusions and actions before, perhaps, the time was right. Speeding along the process of connecting my family together—*this* was my goal. For Jinx, it was the right thing, the *only* thing to do: to speak the truth and possibly sacrifice everything to do it.

Hoping my renewed relationship with Jinx would facilitate a better connection with my mother, I summoned up my courage and made the call, telling myself I owed it to Jinx. My parents and Jinx had not spoken for many years, and although I was afraid, I would try my mother one more time. What did I have to lose, after all?

The truth does not set you free. It only makes you truthful.

"Mom, how are you?"

"Fine, honey. What's happening down there in New York?"

"Oh, nothing much, just concerts and stuff."

"What about the shows? Are you still doing lots of them?"

My mother saw Broadway shows as the musical equivalent of secretarial work. She got comfort and reassurance from her impression that the show gigs looked like "steady" work. It wasn't my month-long European tours with the Orpheus Chamber Orchestra she was impressed with but rather the grind-'em-out shows like *Beauty and the Beast* and *Phantom of the Opera* that I'd subbed on hundreds of times.

"Yeah, the shows are fine. Mom, there's something I need to tell you."

"Okay, honey."

"Well…I've been in touch with Jinx."

That pause. For the ages. I waited.

"Really."

"Yeah. And…um…we've seen each other."

"Really? Where?"

"I've traveled to Florida a few times. She lives in Miami Beach now. She seems to be doing pretty well...."

"Really."

"Yeah. And, um, I was afraid to tell you because I thought you might get mad."

"How long has this been going on? I mean, how many trips?"

"About five months. I've gone down three times."

"Really."

"And she's changed and all. She's off drugs now...."

"Really? Is that so? Well, I can't say I'm happy about this, Marcia. I just think it's wrong to dredge up the past. Your father and I did everything humanly possible for that girl. We bent over backwards to provide for you girls. We treated you exactly the same. *Exactly* the same. And she was just a disaster: she never appreciated what we did for her, she *destroyed* the family—what happened is on her back. I wish her well, I truly do, but she made her bed—I tell you, she made her own bed...."

That phrase—"made her bed"—rang off-pitch, tinny and strident. Sitting in my apartment on my *own* bed, I drifted off, half listening to her rant of myriad justifications. The odd thing was, I'd made *my* bed perfectly for years. My mother held the treatment of beds in high esteem: a neat and clean home, with a *bed* that was perfectly made up *every single morning*—that was how you conquered the world, according to my mother.

Jinx didn't agree. In fact, while she was growing up, her bedroom had always been a wreck—stuff strewn from here to there. As my mother continued to blather on in the background, I struggled to reconcile how it could possibly be that Jinx had "made her bed," figuratively and in reality.

Zoom—I was flat on my back, lying on the carpet of childlike accommodation in Pittsfield, Massachusetts, dodging my mother's whapping electrical cord. The rug was no longer velvet-cut pile but rather a commercial remnant made of viscose. It scratched, and I jumped. Those primordial fighting hormones were stitched into my sinewy muscles from the time when I pummeled Bruce several months earlier with Roth and Austen. An animal instinct began to rage inside me with an urge to defy this woman—the primal woman of my life. Not Kirsten. My *mother.* And this time, for my sister.

I threw myself onto her Pittsfield bed.

"Mom, *please.* What are you *talking* about? You *didn't* treat us the same!"

"We most certainly *did.*"

"Oh, *please!* Father used to beat Jinx up! How do you call *that* treating us the same?"

Silence. Her next words fired back with a pistol whip, the sequel to walking away from a restaurant table, splattering me onto the carpeted gravel of the freshly paved blacktop of 23rd Street.

"I really can't talk about this now."

The truth was just the truth, nothing more. It lay there like a weightless speck of dust to be brushed off the lapel of a coat. And the brilliant clarity of this truth cast its ugly beam of light through a Hoover-like telephone cord, terminating in my hand with a snap.

That *click.* That monstrously soft sound echoed as I wondered how I was going to negotiate my life from now on. Surely she would call back. Perched on my perfectly made bed, I waited for two hours, until 7:15 p.m., the latest possible time I could leave my apartment and still make the 8:00 p.m. downbeat of the show scheduled for that evening. I played *Beauty and the Beast* in a stupor. I was made to wait one full year for her to call back.

It proved to be a busy 364 days.

I received a letter from my father, stating that my mother was the most loving and sensitive woman on the planet. I slept. I won an award from the League of Composers/ISCM and was given a grant to fund an oboe recital, for which I commissioned two new works and performed them at the Weill Recital Hall at Carnegie Hall. I was reviewed in the *New York Times* as "a first-rate artist." I played the American premiere of Elliott Carter's *A 6 Letter Letter*. My father called, informing me via my answering machine that he'd hired a private detective to investigate Jinx and that she was indeed a "bad person," not to be trusted. (So *that's* what those strange hang-ups were: my father disconnecting until he reached my machine.) I continued to nap endlessly. I performed the Strauss Oboe Concerto. I dreamed. I traveled to Europe and throughout the United States, performing with orchestras and chamber music groups. I received another letter from my father—he'd never beaten up my sister, it said, and I was, in effect, crazy, delusional, and an enormous pain in the ass. I slept my Hades-like sleep.

Famous

You meet Rick, a keyboard player, at the Broadway show The Secret Garden. *He's a jazz pianist in real life, and you can relate, being a classical player in real life, because all the disparate disciplines of musicians coalesce on Broadway. Now both of you are standing on a rural road in northern New Jersey, at the bottom of the long driveway leading up to jazz pianist Keith Jarrett's house. You've been hired to perform Keith Jarrett's Adagio for Oboe and String Orchestra at Lincoln Center. And you've invited Rick along to provide the piano accompaniment as you begin the first preliminary rehearsal with Keith, one of the greatest musicians of the twentieth century—the man who played with Miles and virtually every other living icon of the jazz world.*

When the word got out at the show that you had been offered this opportunity with Keith, Rick had immediately jumped in to offer to play the orchestral reduction on piano, and you agreed to bring him along. Rick is a fine jazz pianist and a huge fan of Keith Jarrett. Who wouldn't be? Everyone knows Keith's famous albums: The Köln Concert, Paris Concert, *and* Vienna Concert.

Just how superfamous he is, though, really hits home when

you drive up to his house. About twenty people are hanging out at the end of the driveway, taking photographs. They can't even see the house—or Keith, for that matter—but the fans are there. Your heart races a bit. As you drive up the long driveway, the paparazzi follow you for a while and then drop back, knowing the limits.

You walk into the studio, edgy and shy. You've not met Keith before. He's heard your playing on tape and has engaged you based on that alone. Rick is beside himself, eager for the chance to meet and play for his hero. You warm up a bit, and Rick settles in at the piano in Keith's state-of-the-art recording studio at the back of his house.

The concerto is not difficult technically, and the bulk of the rehearsal is spent on sound, musical gesture, and pacing. At the end of the three hours, Keith relaxes, pleased with what he hears. You breathe a sigh of relief, and Rick gets to spend a few minutes chatting about jazz with his idol.

You perform the New York premiere at Lincoln Center and then at a few other venues, all in preparation for the recording. Manfred Eicher, the founder and head of ECM Records, leaves you alone during the recording sessions, focusing for the most part on how to best capture your sound. The disc gets played frequently on the radio for many years after you record it.

The Letter

THE SEASONS ROUNDED home base. But I was no longer that silent, rigid girl.

"Marcia, it's your mother calling."

"Well. It's about time."

"You don't have to be snippy about it."

"No? How should I be? What would you have me say? Are you kidding me, Mother? You're a year too late, and *I just don't understand!*"

Every single day for a year might have been *the* day—when I could take back the truth of my words, reset the clocks, and put my world in reverse gear. In short, apologize to her. That was my secret intention: to get her back any way I could. But on the 365th day, she pushed me off the tracks she built. The teakettle stopper busted out, and my rage boiled over, scalding my shaking hands as I held the phone receiver a few inches from my mouth. I screeched into the mouthpiece and even surprised myself with my fury. It was as if the words sat right at my throat, ready to be gagged up, coughed out—encouraged by the slightest microscopic spec of the dust of truth that blew my way.

Silence.

"Mother?"

"Honey. I'm calling you *now*."

"Yeah, well. This is just unacceptable. All *year* I waited for you to call me. You hung up on me. You turned your back on me. *Again!* And I got those crazy letters from Father. Those *poisonous* letters. That *coward*."

"What letters? I don't know what you're talking about. But it doesn't matter, all of that. Can't we just move on from this? That's why I'm calling, honey. Let's just start *fresh*."

"No way. No. You can't just dust it up as if nothing happened. Not this time. We need help, Mother. I want to get into medi-ation or therapy with you....Just you and me. We could do an intensive weekend thing. You don't have to lift a finger. I'll make all the arrangements. I'll even come to *you*."

"Don't you think that's a bit drastic? We really don't need to dredge up the past. There's nothing to be gained by that, honey. It accomplishes nothing. Don't you see that? Let's just get past this."

"It's what *I* need, Mother. Don't you see *that?*"

She raised the specter, her age-old concern:

"But therapy will cost a fortune. It can be *very* expensive— hundreds, *maybe thousands,* of dollars. We can't afford that."

"*I'll* pay for it."

"Please, honey. Be serious. *You* can't afford that."

"I *am* serious, and you have no *idea* how much money I have. I'm just saying that you can't refuse because of the expense. That will *not* be the reason to refuse me. Us."

I hesitated a bit, and for a second all I wanted to do was hit the bed hard. We were deep into her money territory, and I knew it was all over.

Now, sitting on the edge of my bed, I stared at my feet. My

toes curled up and pointed into each other—pigeon-toed, like a four-year-old girl. Feeling my shoulders slump, I was unsure if I was four or eighty-four. She was so powerful—and all because she simply held herself back. All the information I sought about her in yearbooks never told me what I really wanted to know. All her secrets, and was I ever, just once, part of them?

"Mom. *Please.* I'm begging you to do this for me. I'm on my *knees.* You won't be sorry; I'll make it all fine. But we need a chance to work it out with a professional. We can't do this on our own. Can't you see that? Please. Just give it a chance. *Please.*"

"I don't know.…I feel like you're going to attack me, and I won't be able to get away."

"Okay. Okay. I *understand* that. But I won't, I promise. And you can leave any time you want. I'll tell the therapist that you can walk out at any time. I'll set it up, and if you spend five minutes in the session and walk out, I *promise* that will be okay. But you won't regret it. *I promise. I'll make it good for you.* I'll make sure that you're *protected.*"

She was silent, and for a few seconds I thought she'd hung up on me.

"Mother?"

"I'm here."

Ah. I'd played it wrong, once again. Raw and lost, I was so small.

"*Please…Mother…*won't you do this for me? I'm really *begging* you.…"

My voice trailed off. My hoarse pleading and whimpering sounded like those of a wounded dog in the middle of the road, baying for a truck to come and finish her off.

"I'll have to think about it."

"Okay. But when will you give me your answer?"

"I don't know. Just let me think about it for a while."

A week later I received a note card from her. Van Gogh's *The Bedroom*.

Dear Marcia—

I cannot do this for you.

Mother

I'd sung a song for my mother. I shrieked that melody, using the full force of my training to compel her to sing back. I used my diaphragm the way Adelweird taught me to, projecting my sound with my very best breath of air. My song was repeated in a billion variations for those ten minutes I had to convince her to love me; to come and take a chance with me; to finally try to fix things. For those ten minutes, as I flopped back and forth through all the keys of Western music and in every polyrhythm known to the greatest of drummers, I saw that the power of my talent was inadequate; that my very essence was of no consequence. I might as well have been deaf and dumb and blind. Because I did not seem to matter to my mother.

That song would float in the air for seven more years. I heard it echoing in the distance as I counted the anniversaries and waited for some antiphonal response. My mother had no song for me.

Kirsten sang:

In the wafting Universe of the World-Breath—
drown.

Grass

You lie on your back. Tufts of green grass scratch your neck as you look up into the cloudy sky. A few helicopters circle Yankee Stadium as twenty thousand adoring Korean fans sway back and forth in perfect unison, singing the classic American song "You Are My Sunshine" nonstop for five straight hours. Since 6:00 a.m., for eight hours now, they've been waiting for their True Father, the Reverend Sun Myung Moon. We musicians have long since left the orchestra platform and are lounging all over the field, some in the outfield, some at home plate. When you head into the dugout from time to time to use the facilities, you find young girls lined up in the corridors sobbing uncontrollably. They were hoping their True Father would arrive in one of the helicopters. He does not.

They feed you, as one of the musicians, a sandwich and a soda, but the twenty thousand worshippers have eaten nothing. You offer an orange to one small girl, who just shakes her head rapidly while she rocks back and forth in some kind of self-comforting titration. These girls—perfectly made up, neatly dressed, wildly obedient, and crying for their True Father, who never appears. Are all parents simply a fantasy? All seems lost.

Suddenly they call the job, and you load into the orchestra bus, which takes you back to Carroll Studios, on West 41st Street. You never played a note of the carefully rehearsed concert, but your heart aches as if you had just heard a performance of Mozart's Requiem. *Twenty thousand souls just died, including the small girl you spoke to, whose tears stay with you for many weeks. Such heartfelt yet unrequited devotion is something you know about.*

Road Trip

THE CAR WINDOW was cracked open. The breeze felt good, bracing; but it was beginning to rain—just a mist on my face. Sitting in the backseat of a car was preferable to the musicians' bus. Buses make me queasy, so I jumped at the chance to get in a car with a few of my colleagues. Traveling south on the Taconic State Parkway, after an Orpheus Chamber Orchestra concert at the Troy Savings Bank Music Hall near Albany, New York, I settled in for the postconcert four-hour ride home. We'd stopped off at a Wawa to get doughnuts and sodas. I would reach my apartment sometime around 3 a.m.

The Troy music hall has acoustics on par with Carnegie Hall and has been for years an esteemed venue for classical music recordings, not to mention concerts. Orpheus would repeat this same concert at Carnegie Hall in a week. During this performance set, I had been subbing for the brilliant oboist whom I sat next to on my very first union job, many years ago.

The misty rain suddenly turned to drops, and I rolled up the window. Now, with the car quiet, I listened to my front-seat colleagues chatting about their kids.

"He's very good at engineering principles, apparently. At least that's what his science teacher tells us. God, I can't even put Legos together....I have no idea where he gets the knack. Some ancient dinosaur gene, no doubt. And certainly on my husband's side."

"I *know*. It's like a miracle—they have talents and interests that wouldn't occur to you, and then all of a sudden they start talking about *careers* and what they want to *do with their lives*. So different from when we were young. All we wanted to do was play music."

"Marcia, are there any doughnuts left?"

"Sure—powdered sugar? Kind of messy."

"Fine."

I passed the napkin-wrapped doughnut into the front seat. The rain lightened up, and I cracked the window again. No one was on the highway, and as we whizzed by, I noticed bright red deer eyes on the side of the road, blurred like time-lapsed beacons. My head lolled on the half-open window glass. I was engrossed in their far-flung topics—moms curious about their children; mothers considering deep love as if from a distance.

"My mother thinks I should enroll him in some kind of advanced class for science. But it's not just science—he likes to look inside of stuff. Last week he took my sewing machine apart and then put it back together, not a screw left over. I didn't even notice it until I saw that the dust around the machine had been disturbed. And then I saw that the machine was backwards on the table—*then* he fessed up."

"Marcia, you sounded great tonight, by the way."

"Yeah, you really did. So much great stuff for you in the Schoenberg."

"Thanks."

We'd performed the Kammersymphonie no. 1, op. 9, that evening.

"But my mother's really pushing this gifted thing. Not too sure how I feel about it. What about a balance? I don't want him to get locked into anything at this age, because you never know what might surface later. God, honestly? I just pray that he's happy."

"Happy sounds simple enough. Your mother sounds so involved, though. I mean, is she overbearing and intrusive?"

"No, not at all. And I need it because I really feel *clueless*. I don't know what I'd do without her, especially now that my son is showing these signs of real talent. But you're right, she *does* have the rag in the mouth about it. Not in a bad way: it's just that she's so damned proud of him. She says *her* grandfather was a civil engineer.... So maybe the genes *are* on both sides and skipped a few generations. He loves her to bits, too. She sings Mozart arias to him at bedtime."

"That's so sweet! *That* gene didn't skip!"

"I don't know—it's kind of embarrassing. But I guess it could be worse...."

The misty rain mixed with the salt from my silent tears. It could, indeed, be much worse.

The Taconic always seemed pitch dark late at night, more than other highways. We'd not seen cars driving in the other direction for a while, so my friend switched on the high beams. Now we could easily see the deer, whole families chowing down in the dark until the headlights startled them. The chatter in the front seat died down—this lull was somehow welcomed. My friend turned on the radio, finding a classical station after some static-filled dialing. We happened upon the last five minutes of *Siegfried Idyll*. For the love of a child.

Two hundred miles east, a parallel highway ran southward. My mother was somewhere over in that direction—to my left. We lived hundreds of miles apart, but still next to the same ocean, still in the same time zone. If she were to come to me, I knew just how it might work....

She would begin on I-95 at Hampton Falls, near Stratham, New Hampshire, where she and my father lived. Traveling south, my mother would have the option of turning right prematurely onto I-495 toward Haverhill and Lowell, Massachusetts. This would, in effect, cut off a large portion of I-95, to save travel time as she rounded Boston, heading to all points south. But I gave due respect to my mother and her aversions and particular eccentricities. An eventual left-hand turn in order to get back onto I-95 was not possible.

The National Highway System would be kind to my mother as she traveled down the East Coast. Stretching her legs in front of her, her lovely knees emerging from just below the hem of her shirtwaist dress, she would press down on the accelerator. Southward now—through Massachusetts and into Connecticut toward Danbury.

A few months before, I'd played a pops concert in Danbury, Connecticut, at an outdoor venue a few miles off I-84. We were backing up the folk-pop singer Judy Collins. We'd had a truly miserable afternoon rehearsal, with the late setting sun blazing directly into our eyes and the temperature soaring into the nineties; the humidity must have topped off at a sopping 100 percent. The stage, cantilevered over a man-made pond, begat swarms of bugs, both biting and benign. Valiantly trying to make music, we smacked a mosquito every ten notes or so. Judy hung on like a pro.

Between the bug swats and the slippery sweat, I couldn't seem to get comfortable. Nature didn't intend for music to be made under such debilitating conditions. Looking to my right, I was about to bark out an angry rant to the flutist next to me—certainly a generally sympathetic listener on the topic of inhumane performing conditions. But I never got the words out, because I was startled to notice that he was intently staring at my bare knees: inspecting them, really.

He reached down and gently brushed the skin above my knee with his forefinger.

"Is your skin always like this?"

"What do you mean? Like what?"

"Smooth, like porcelain. I've never seen such soft skin before. Sorry. I just had to touch it."

I stared at him. How very observant he was. I smiled, and, encouraged, he repeated the question.

"Is your skin always like this?"

"Yes. Yes, it is."

Finally. Someone had noticed. In that very instant, I was tenderly and unabashedly connected to my mother, her wonderfully curved legs, but more specifically her very special knees. I looked nothing like her, but we must have shared a wondrously rare, recessive gene: *the skin above my knee.*

Judy began singing "Suzanne" by Leonard Cohen, and I was jarred out of my musings on the Butler family genetic helix. The song floats over the subject of suicide.

As if a strong magnetic force had pulled me down, all at once my head dropped onto my soft knees. I rubbed my forehead into the skin as I sobbed. The orchestra played on.

Relathered by my tears, the Jergens lotion I had applied earlier in the day (the same brand my mother always used) gave off its sickening scent, snapping my head upright again like a whiff of smelling salts. I rejoined the orchestra, Suzanne, and Judy as she sang:

And you want to travel with her
And you want to travel blind....

Jolting me from my Danbury reverie, our car veered sharply away from a doe that was too close to the road. The Taconic was too narrow, really, to accommodate cars and families of deer. As *Siegfried* concluded, my friends took up their earlier topic again.

"What about your mother? You're a bit older, right? Did she dote on your kids?"

"Not really....She had some health problems when my kids were young, so we missed all that. But she sure makes up for it now, because she can't seem to keep her nose out of my daughter's love life. No boundaries *at all.* My daughter says her grandma should write a how-to book on all the right things to do to nab a husband, a step-by-step tutorial on exactly how to get someone to love you. Forever, of course."

A thin pamphlet on love would do. I closed my eyes and saw her pass Danbury.

Now, Mother. Now you can turn. And here is how: your hands are on the steering wheel at the ten and two positions. You must grip the wheel in a determined yet relaxed manner. You see the first of many large green signs ahead of you. You depress the brake pedal with your foot, which is connected to your lovely calf, which in turn resolves at the soft skin above your knee. You slow down gradually, and over the next five miles, you prepare to make the turn that will deliver you to my door. As you come up to the last of the green signs for the exit you'll need to take, you pass by. You've managed to brake in preparation, but you don't turn. Instead you accelerate and drive southward, past the 59th Street Bridge, past the Midtown Tunnel, and proceed to all points south.

I gaze into the distance, straining, and my eyes bore into the back of your head. Startled, I remember that my father always had the wheel when you took road trips. My father drove by all the signs.

We entered the 2:00 a.m. light traffic flow coming down from the Bronx. The rough city roads shook me.

"Marcia, should I take I-95 into Manhattan and then drive into Queens by the Midtown Tunnel? Or the 59th Street Bridge? What's the best way?"

Feeling groggy, I bolted forward in my seat.

"Those are both left-hand turns. Is that okay with you?"

"Of course….Either is fine. But which is shortest?"

"Oh, the 59th Street Bridge. That's the straightest shot. There's no toll. And fewer turns."

You careened right by my house. And I was standing very still with my eyes closed; standing and waiting for you; singing to you. And listening.

What does love look like? Is it Kirsten's voice? A turn signal on a car? Is it a black-and-white dress? Is it the back of your head? A vacuum cleaner? Is it Shalimar perfume? Is it Isolde's words? Is it a Camel cigarette? Whitney? A child whom I aborted? André

Watts? Vikki Carr? My knee or your knee? Is it glass? A poem?
Is it the entire length of I-95 and the East Coast of the United
States of America?

Kirsten sang:

Do I alone hear this melody…

168 Hours

For freelancers, opportunities for big concerts are limited to three times a week: Friday night, Saturday night, and Sunday afternoon. Many orchestras plan their seasons without consulting one another—wouldn't it be nice if they did? So there is a lot of overlap between concert series. And you need to make as much money as possible, so as a musician you never say no to a gig. Ever. So here goes . . .

You wake up on Monday and go into your studio, warm up, and start one new reed. Adelweird taught you to start one new reed a day—and you still follow his laws of oboe playing. One new reed a day, and you won't, in theory, have reed problems. Unless the cane is shitty.

Then you head out for a 10:00 a.m.–1:00 p.m. rehearsal for the upcoming Friday night concert. That afternoon at home, you practice for about an hour on the music to be performed during the Saturday night and Sunday afternoon concert set.

That evening you play a Broadway show—Phantom of the Opera.

On Tuesday you have a double rehearsal, 10:00–1:00 and

217

3:00–5:30, for the Saturday-Sunday concert set. You play a different Broadway show that night: Beauty and the Beast.

On Wednesday you practice your concert music in the morning and start a reed. You work on the reed started that Monday, hoping it might be okay for one of the concerts. You play the matinee of Beauty and the Beast, *and then you play* The King and I *that night. You use older reeds for the Broadway shows because you are saving the good ones for the concerts. Also, playing older reeds is easier on the "chops" (mouth).*

On Thursday you have a rehearsal at Alice Tully Hall at Lincoln Center from 1:00 p.m. to 4:00 p.m. for the Friday night concert. That morning, you start a new reed and continue to refine and work on the others. At this point you're playing the new reeds in the rehearsals to see if they'll be good enough for concerts. Two are promising. You have Thursday night free.

But the weather changes, and it starts to rain. It has been dry and sunny all week. Weather and humidity drastically change the reeds, including those you've been making and playing on. So instead of relaxing on Thursday night, you start three new reeds so that you'll be prepared if the ones started earlier, during dry weather, don't work.

On Friday it's still raining, so you rise early and check out all your reeds, and you practice a little. You have a 10:00–1:00 dress rehearsal for the evening concert. Then you go home and rest for a few hours. You play the concert on a reed that is good but not great. Tully is a nice hall, but you are not crazy about the way the reed sounds there. It sounded better in the rehearsal studio. Oh, well. No one notices, really: it is just an internal comfort level. You are a perfectionist and have the inner critic from hell, as most musicians do.

On Saturday you drive up to Connecticut, where the weekend concerts are. You play a rehearsal in the morning, a dress rehearsal in the afternoon, and then the concert at night. You rotate the reeds because you don't want to use up the really good one in the rehearsals unless it's absolutely necessary.

Truly exhausted after the concert, you drive home and try to sleep late on Sunday morning.

After Sunday breakfast, you drive to Connecticut for the 3:00 p.m. repeat concert and decide at the last minute to use a different reed because the weather has gone dry again and everything has shifted. The traffic back to the city from Connecticut is horrendous, and you don't get home until 8:00 p.m. But you eat dinner and go into the studio at 10:00 p.m. to start a reed.

The next morning, Monday, you have a day off—but not really. You need to gouge cane and make reeds and practice for the music coming up this week. And you get a last-minute call for a Broadway show that night: Miss Saigon.

Your answer is yes. Always.

The Fallen

THE LADY SANG, but not for me.

In 1999, Jinx was diagnosed with tongue cancer. My mother swarmed to her like a drone to a queen. That scene of so many years ago at Bellevue Hospital, when Jinx was laid out in a suicidal coma-sleep, was replayed in Miami Beach. Now years later and wide awake, Jinx accepted all the kindness and attention finally coming her way. With frequent phone calls, a few visits, and lots of money—all the usual hallmarks of a concerned family—my mother came to the rescue of her twice-fallen yodeling Heidi.

Cancer seemed to be the great leveler. I would have traded places with Jinx in a nanosecond, just as I would have at Bellevue. I would have taken on a deadly disease if that were the perfect accompaniment for my mother's aria. Sitting in the corner of Jinx's living room during one of my many visits to Florida while she endured her treatments, I wore the dunce cap of a hidden sister, listening to a one-sided phone conversation. As I eavesdropped, it was clear that Jinx was lapping up the attention, but she never once mentioned my presence. Clearly it was best for me to remain invisible, offstage.

After a few months, I gingerly broached the elephant in the room.

"Jinx, this is all feeling pretty weird. The last time I was in Miami, I was sitting right there when Mother called. You didn't even acknowledge that I was in the same room with you. And you've done this from the beginning, ever since you got sick and they showed up. Can't you say something to Mother? You know I haven't heard a word from her in seven years. Can't you stick up for me? It feels as if you're hiding me. I really don't get this."

I was at the pay phone in the backstage area in between the matinee and the evening performance of *Beauty and the Beast*. Ratty sofas were scattered throughout the backstage catacombs of the theater, and directly after the matinee I usually made a beeline for one of them and took a nap for an hour. Waking that afternoon, I'd headed for the pay phone in a corner by the ladies' room and made my daily check-in call to Jinx.

"I'll bring it up, but not now. It's not the right time."

"But *when?*"

Her tone began to change, reminding me of her defiance toward my father, years ago.

"I don't know. It's just not the right time. That's all."

"But she's admitted to all the stuff Father did to you; all that stuff she wouldn't talk to me about. She denied it all to me. And now, suddenly she's on board—but for you."

There was silence on the other end of the line. I felt her weighing her options. Jinx was crafty. I'd seen her work this new system during the last few months of her illness. I heard her tell one person one thing and another person something completely different—parents and friends alike.

Silence.

Uncomfortable, I broke in with additional propping up.

"I'm happy for you; don't get me wrong. This is what's supposed to happen in families—somebody gets sick, and the troops gather. But why can't you stand up for me? Why?"

"Marcia, it's not *about* you. This is about *me*, and I will talk to her when I'm ready. I'm just not going to rock that boat right now."

"But what do you have to lose? You've got them in your pocket now. Why *not*, for God's sake?"

"Marcia, stop it! *I'm* the one with the cancer!"

She was screaming now. I didn't dare raise my voice, because I was in the theater at a public phone. But I couldn't let it slide. She *had* to understand me.

"I know. I know you have cancer. But I stood by you, and I don't have a family now because of that. I sacrificed *everything* for you. It's been seven years now. Don't you see that? You *must* see that."

"Well, now *I've* got them, and I've got to do this the way I want. Because they *owe* me."

I considered her reasoning and her very nature. A woman who had been brutally thrown away by her parents at a young age couldn't be expected to know or understand anything about loyalty. *I* knew about true loyalty. *I* was the one who went back and back—with Steve and Bruce and my mother and my father. And now with Jinx.

"They *owe* me."

She repeated her simple defense, and suddenly it all made sense. As a sober adult, Jinx still lived on the fundamentals of "getting over" and "getting back" and certainly settling scores. As money and attention came her way, she headed, zombielike, in that direction. Once, I was in her corner, sacrificing the bout for her. Now she was ill and could safely cast me aside and head for the gilded majority, who happened to be the parents we both longed for. And they really *did* owe her. How could I argue with that logic? Who could blame her?

Standing in the corner, hanging onto the pay-phone box, I let myself slide down onto my haunches and quietly cried into the phone. She reiterated her intended revenge.

"They *owe* me. And they're going to pay."

"But don't you see? If you just say something, then she would *know* that I'm here, and then *I* would have a chance, too. Mother would accept me if it came from you. I *know* she would...."

I heard her sigh heavily, with exasperation. Then I heard the roar of a wounded animal.

"Marcia, *shut the fuck up!!* Grow up and just leave me alone."

The phone went dead. Without thinking, I called her back, but she didn't give me a chance to utter a word.

"You *bitch,* fucking leave me alone. Don't call me again."

Decapitated again, I redialed. The line went dead with that unnerving fast beeping signal. She'd yanked the cord from the socket.

Sitting on the floor, deep in the catacombs of a Broadway theater, I turned again into a corner where two walls met at ninety degrees. I wasn't really certain who was the mother or the child in my relationship with Jinx; we vacillated with an influx of support and need, depending on our specific vulnerabilities, throughout the last seven years of our relationship. As I silently wept the bitterest tears known to womankind, every nerve in my body went horribly numb, and a sense memory came up, choking my throat closed. I saw Jinx as my mother snapping yet one more cord away from me. Another mother who was killing me or simply turning her back on me for reasons I still could not yet fathom.

I sat in my ancient yet familiar crouched position and listened to the dressers and wardrobe ladies in the next room talk about their gardens and their husbands and their wonderfully simple lives. Actresses and makeup artists quietly walked past to use the restroom. I heard their bladders being emptied and their hands being washed. The towels being pulled down, the trashcan lid creaking open and slamming shut. A few of the orchestra ladies brushed their hands over my hair as they passed me on their way out.

I heard the announcement: "Half hour, ladies and gentlemen. Half hour. It is half an hour till the eight o'clock performance. For this performance, so-and-so will be in for so-and-so. So-and-so will be in for so-and-so. Half hour, ladies and gentlemen, half hour. It is now half hour."

I had a show to play. Still shaky, I stood up, slipped into the ladies' room, emptied my bladder, washed my face and hands, and entered the pit. I called in the performance.

Back at home after the show, crawling into my bed, I prayed for a deep sleep to release me. But my eyes would not close, and my mind would not quiet down. I was without a mother and father, and now I was without a sister.

Space

Seated inside a prestigious church on the Upper East Side of New York City, you prepare to begin a concert marathon of music called the St. Matthew Passion *by Johann Sebastian Bach, telling the story of Jesus's death on the cross. You're not religious, yet religious content is immaterial to the profundity of the music. Nearly three hours long, the work requires you to play all three instruments in the oboe family: the oboe; the oboe d'amore, pitched a third below the oboe; and the English horn, pitched a fifth below the oboe. And yes, you have to make different reeds for each instrument.*

For weeks, you prepare. You make lots of reeds in order to get exactly the right ones—those that will hold up and have the endurance necessary to perform this marathon work. Because it has numerous solo arias for the oboe, the Passion *gives you a prominent voice. It's like playing a concerto, many concertos, over the span of a three-hour concert. You want to put your own stamp of artistry on it yet at the same time be in service to the master composer of all time: Bach.*

But there's the endurance issue that worries you—and worries every oboist. Your mouth, your embouchure, which is the position of the mouth around the reed, has built up rigid, strong muscles over time, and you can surely play for long periods. But it is just muscle, after all, and you do get tired on occasion. And that is not a happy sensation, especially during a concert. The St. Matthew Passion *tests the endurance of all oboists.*

You are now into the performance at about the two-and-a-half-hour mark. Jesus, hanging on the cross, has died a few minutes before. Your right arm begins to go tingly and numb. The heavy weight of the English horn and the position of your right arm cause this. You are about to play the big chorus with bass solo and orchestra, which is one of your favorite sections. But your mouth is extremely tired, and you are very worried that you won't be able to get through the piece. Or even hold up your instrument.

The music restarts; you begin. The whole orchestra, and the chorus and the soloists, must sense the strain of the evening. Then, what feels like a cloud of energy begins to gather at your feet, milky and vaporous. And as you play, this cloud spreads across the floor and envelops the whole orchestra. And you are aware that not only do you have the energy required to play, your mouth also feels as if it is not even on your face. Your right arm is suspended as if by an invisible sling. And as you play and notice these unusual sensations, you look around the orchestra and imagine that every person playing is buoyed by the same incredible energy and life force. And you're hearing all the notes, every single note, being played and sung by everyone. But not only that: you also hear or sense all the spaces between the notes.

You suddenly understand that there is no separation or distinction between the notes, the spaces between the notes, and the people playing the notes and the people listening to the notes and the church and the street and the city and the earth. Maybe even the universe. You understand in this very brief period of time that Bach's intimate portrayal of the death of Jesus is one way to become connected to the universe. And you hold on to this for the rest of the concert. As you silently leave the stage after the concert, you look at the other musicians, wondering if they, too, understood or sensed what happened. It is art and it is love, communicated through the soul of Johann Sebastian Bach.

Donna

I STEPPED INTO the elevator, and my jaw dropped. Donna Summer, diminutive, stood in the corner. She quickly looked upward and gazed at the nothingness of the ceiling. Where else could she look? Starstruck, I gawked. I relished the time in the slow lift (and of course all sense of time was absurdly distorted now, as if in a dry-ice disco dream) just to be in her presence and resurrect the lyrics to "MacArthur Park" in my music-memory. "Someone left the cake out in the rain" thrilled and confounded me (and everyone else) when I first heard the song. Who would be so careless? And why, pray tell, did the cake take so long to bake? Then there was that missing recipe. Metaphor was lost to me in the late 1970s. But now, in spring of 2000, I felt proud that *finally*—sadly wiser, certainly older—I understood Donna's song.

The words were on the tip of my tongue: "Oh, Donna…you'll never know how…" But no; I held it back. Out of respect. The gawking was enough. The fifth floor came, the doors opened, and as she exited, with a red scarf whipping behind her, she looked back at me and smiled. How I loved Donna Summer and her endless last dance.

I continued to the seventh floor of Roosevelt Hospital. Stepping inside the well-lit yet cozy room, I plopped down and presented my arm, elbow down, vein side up. The nice male nurse strapped it tightly onto the arm of the recliner with thick tape. After he tapped the area a few times with his fingers, the vein at the crease of my elbow conveniently popped up.

"Are you ready?"

"Yup: let 'er rip."

"Okay, here goes. Hold still, Marcia. Don't…you…move…"

I squeezed my eyes shut and held my breath. Not that doing those two things would help. This was my third injection, and I knew the drill; still, I didn't want to look or breathe. It was important that I not move an inch while I endured the excruciating sixty seconds it took for him to inject ruby-red Adriamycin into my vein. You can't slow-drip the drug, because it is so caustic it'll breach the vein and burn out surrounding tissue immediately. That's why they call it the Big Red Push. And then there was my heart, any heart, which can't take more than six doses in a given lifetime.

Almost six months to the day after Jinx slammed the phone down, I was diagnosed with invasive breast cancer. And the reason Donna Summer was staring at the ceiling was most likely not because she wanted to avoid a conversation with an adoring fan but because I was bald. Most people can't look at bald women. I discovered *that* three weeks previously, when my hair began to fall out during the intermission of a concert. I finished the concert semi-bald. That's when I began to notice uncomfortable, averted glances.

I squirmed in the recliner, trying not to pant.

"Are you okay?"

"No. Give me the bucket. *Fast.*"

Charles, the nurse, while still proceeding with the injection, quickly leaned down, picked up the small bucket, and slid it under my chin. I waited, but nothing came up. I supposed that was a good thing, because I had to get to a rehearsal in an hour.

"False alarm, Charles."

I began to sweat, and tears came to my eyes. I couldn't get through these damned injections without whimpering.

"Okay, we're almost done now. Just a few more drops…"

Charles pulled out the syringe, unstrapped my arm, and walked away. I wept like a baby.

Perhaps cancer had been growing inside me as far back as forty years earlier, burrowing deep into my right breast. I imagined those hideous cells hiding behind my nipple, waiting to multiply from the days I ran giggling behind the mosquito trucks in Pittsfield, Massachusetts, inhaling the fairy dust of DDT in the 1960s of my childhood. The arrival of the truck, at about 7:00 p.m., when mosquitoes are at their most ferocious, was something to look forward to—like going for an ice cream cone. Both activities broke the heat of the day. I ran in my pajamas so I could slip directly into bed while the cooling, killer mist continued to chill my body.

My luck-of-the-draw genes might have also been the culprits, but there was no family history of breast cancer. What did it matter? Cancer is cancer, and I set about taking the disease in hand, demolishing it with surgery, six pushes of red chemotherapy, and then topping it all off with forty consecutive skin-blistering doses of radiation.

I did have compassionate friends, including a few special ones who came to my aid during my diagnosis and treatment; also the dear musicians with whom I'd spent many years playing my heart out. My own tribe of oboists gathered around, made calls, and ensured that I was covered in case I was suddenly too ill for rehearsals or concerts. But I rarely missed a concert or even a beat—literally.

Receiving attention and care was not easy for me. I was surprised and bewildered at first because I assumed that, for the most part, I was not well liked. This perception took hold and festered under my skin well before my years at Mannes. I was certain that I was not worthy of true friendship. Indeed, I wasn't entirely sure what friendship looked like and was wary—suspicious, even—of anyone who would *want* to be my friend at all.

This utter self-disregard was not glaring or outwardly gleaned by others. A good little actress (I'd successfully hidden so much of my life over the years), I presented as a lively, darkly funny, gutter-mouthed, punctual, always prepared, and somewhat outspoken member of the music community. But underneath, I felt dead certain that my well-deserved self-loathing was a catastrophic reality visible for all to see and believe.

When your parents don't speak to you for years at a time, it's hard not to conclude that there must be a valid reason. I was unessential, dispensable, not worth the trouble—not worth even one fight. Wouldn't everyone else see me that way, too? That was *rational* reasoning. My calculating and compartmentalizing mind easily projected my own assumptions onto men, friends, and anyone I met.

But there existed a smoking gun right in my back pocket, and it was loaded with a golden bullet: cancer. I actually saw my cancer diagnosis as fortuitous. Further logic led me to bank on the distinct possibility that my family might come to *my* aid, just as my parents had come to Jinx's aid when she was diagnosed less than a year before. After all, Jinx had also been considered a colossal pain in the ass. I was finally in the correct state of health to *now* warrant their attention. Cancer. Happy days.

With my reasoning solidified, I'd made a plan. A few days after my diagnosis, while I completed testing for the upcoming surgery, I'd dispatched notes to my parents and Jinx. That's what my mother had taught me—any important information should be written in lovely cursive script on a pretty note card and should arrive through the post. I still lived by her rules of comportment. I heard nothing but was still hopeful. Then, two weeks later, while recovering from the operation, I received a Hallmark card in response to one of the notes and ultimately nothing in response to the other. No calls, no urgent footsteps at my door. Silence, again, when I needed a crashing Mahler symphony.

Across the room, Charles sat beside his next victim, preparing to administer the red poison. I blew my nose, wiped my eyes, and thought again about my red-scarfed disco diva. My day was jammed to the gills, so I jumped up, grabbed my oboe, ran to a 10:00–1:00 rehearsal, then played a Broadway show at 2:00 p.m. As I was traveling home on the subway at 5:00 p.m., my stomach felt as if it were inside out, raked raw. The nausea usually held off until the evening after a morning injection, but today it had been a crafty little demon. Just when I thought I'd gotten the "sick schedule" down, my system decided to change course. The second act of the show had been tough to get through.

When I finally arrived home I experienced a brand-new depth of beyond terrible. It wasn't just the nausea but also the skin-crawling reality that I was being pumped with poison. The sensation defies words until you've felt it. Balloons are balloons.

Snowflakes are snowflakes. Red is red. And chemo is chemo. I let the door slam behind me as all the pages in my "childhood journal of firsts" nestled together inside my nude skull.

The phone machine blinked red. But first to the bathroom, then to the kitchen to munch on a few crackers, then to my studio to drop my oboe gear down, then to my reed desk to look at what I'd made the night before. Picking up the reeds one by one, I scrutinized my handiwork as the blinks in the next room nagged at me, pulsing out their backbeat. I wondered who was on the other side of those blinks.

Tired and sick, I decided to forget about practicing and just organize and mentally review my music for the next day's concert. Busying myself with this mundane task took all of ten minutes, but the night ahead loomed large and endless, like the unreachable horizon across a vast sea. My life was full of music, yet I felt empty — with the accelerator pressed to the floor, the engine revving high, but the gear in neutral.

Drawing a hot bath, I sat in the tub until I felt the chill of tepid water, which usually made me dive under my bedcovers and fall asleep instantly. Not tonight — the blinks, now red screaming beacons, lit up the darkened living room. I still had those blinks to negotiate.

After I'd toweled off, I settled on the sofa. My cotton nightgown was badly wrinkled from a starchy flop sweat the night before, and I smoothed it down, trying to tamp the creases out with the palm of my hand. An urge to vomit was close, and I was panting, trying to stave it off, so I threw a blanket over my legs and curled into a fetal position. Perhaps a bit of TV would distract me. No: it all looked ugly and too crisp — loud and meaningless. I clicked it off with a rough gesture and threw the remote to the end of the sofa. It landed on my toe, and I let out a weak yelp.

Finally I was ready to listen. I reached over my head, felt for the top of the machine without looking, found the right button, and pressed down.

"Marcia, do you want a ride this weekend? I can pick you up at the usual place at twelve noon on Saturday. Just let me know tomorrow."

"Hey, Marcia, can you play *Beast* again tomorrow night? I'm still not feeling well enough. Call me in the morning."

"Miss Butler, your dry cleaning has been sitting here for three weeks. Please, come pick it up."

The machine was dark, silent, with the wrong words by the wrong people still jammed inside the plastic box. I lay on the sofa, shivering and perhaps feverish, praying for drowsiness to take me down. Instead the steroids my doctor had prescribed to hold back the nausea (they weren't working) forced me into the graveyard shift: staying awake to think about the *right* words from the *right* people.

That steroid-addled night, as I began to feel achy, with a strange and ugly urgency in my chest, I made long lists of all the words I wanted to hear and lined them up, complete with perfectly inflected intonation. The words might falter at first or, alternatively, come out as run-on sentences. But I'd straighten them out and realign them so they would resemble the melody of a perfect Schubert song. I pushed the lists of potential words through my chemo-fogged brain sieve and tried to make them fewer and easier to say. Those spare, culled-down words, spoken by the *right* people, just might cure my cancer.

Waking with a start a few hours later, I glanced at the clock:

4:00 a.m. At that moment, panting as if a released kinetic energy were in flailing free fall, I felt my rational brain shut down like a citywide blackout. But light was not necessary—or even wanted—because my dark inner gut, that brilliant secondary brain center, had taken over. My belly ached and glowed with a stark and luminous reckoning. I had finally pinpointed what I'd always deeply known, and it took the terrible nadir of a chemotherapy night to clear out any remnant of deluded optimism. I was an awful person—truly bad to the core. *That* was the reason. There was just no other explanation possible. They'd never call. They'd never come.

Still lying on the sofa, I propped myself up and took a good look around. The door to my studio was ajar, and I noticed my oboe resting on the desk. Cane shavings littered the floor. Music volumes sat stacked on a bookshelf. A metronome, a sharpening stone, dozens of reed knives, boxes of French tube cane, and all the detritus of the life of an oboe player—the contents of that room represented everything that had somehow kept me alive or simply sane. Or so I'd thought. I ruefully shook my head in disgust for deluding myself with useless feelings like hoping and wanting; for thinking that words could somehow help me. And for the first time in my life, with my fresh evaluation of who and what I *really* was, I even questioned the power of music.

With no strength in my thin neck tendons, my bald head dropped back, and the tears came, rolling down the sides of my cheeks. I silently sobbed with my mouth open in what must have been a ghoulish expression—an Edvard Munch scream, soundless. Willing myself to regain control, I choked the ache back and swallowed my misery. All I wanted to do was sleep or go numb. Either way, somehow, I went under.

At 6:00 a.m., the day was finally breaking. The sky outside my window had taken on a pink cast—the cusp of a red dawn. Birds were beginning to sing their wake-up song in spite of an anticipated downpour. My feet felt for the rug, and I dug my toes in. I leaned forward, gripped my head, rubbed my hands into the exposed, odd skull skin, and resolved to take a new course of action. I would personify with great precision the woman my mother, my father, and my sister believed me to be—a woman who couldn't be loved, a woman not deserving of *any* words. But to do this I'd need to feel much less, care very little, and rid myself of all the red inside my body. I knew just how I'd do this: I'd slice up my heart, bleed it dry, then rip it to tiny shreds until it floated away with the storm that would come with the bright red morning. No one would *ever* enter my heart again. I'd lock it up in a dark, airless room where the music of words would not resonate within and the color red could not penetrate the walls. And I'd kill off my bloody red heart to do it.

Oh, Donna, let's dance the last dance.

Black

Change is transformative but elusive, like a vague sensation traveling through your mind or body during a specific moment. You may notice that the earth has measurably slowed, or, conversely, the moment might feel like a fleeting gesture, an electrical spark that is quick and harsh but memorable. A shift into new territory, through a life event or a performance, is a far-off goal, never to be fully attained, because you never completely know yourself. It's only through mighty, wearying struggle that you begin to discover a tiny piece of who you are. Where your guts truly reside. That path becomes crystal clear not in what you can do but in what simply cannot be done.

So you sense the universe spinning in black space, out of control, whipping back and forth with unchecked abandon. This energy moves closer to earth; its frenetic movement slows a bit and becomes regulated. It becomes the orbiting of the sun and the moon and the earth. The wind, sea, and tides take over, re-creating this undulation on the planet. The final point of contact is you. You start it all over again with what you create, and that creation is tossed back up, projected into the infinite universe. Who ultimately knows what happens to the sound of an oboe, or Kirsten's voice, or Donna's last dance, or the red of a dawning day?

Emily

WATER SLUICED DOWN my back. Turning around, I stuck my face directly in front of the sharp pinging beads of water. My nude skull was covered with soap. In spite of being bald, I continued with the futile routine of shampooing. I took a deep breath, held it in, and braced myself. Then I twisted the hot handle off, and the water went ice cold. It was torture. I imagined that a cold rinse at the end of my morning shower would energize me after the previous night of terrible reckoning. I needed a distraction from my full-frontal sadness.

I stepped out of the shower, had a big shiver, and caught a glimpse of my dripping body in the mirror on the back of the bathroom door. With my nakedness reflected back at me, how could I not notice that even though I'd lost weight during my treatment, my face was puffy and my belly had developed a new, unattractive paunch? It might have been attributable to lack of exercise; I'd been a runner before the cancer diagnosis. But not now. The ongoing treatment had left me beyond exhausted, achingly sad and now disfigured.

The most disturbing feature I saw was my right breast. It was smaller and higher than the left. Size didn't matter, but I didn't particularly care for this lack of symmetry. Worse, the penguin-beak scar was still there. Over the years, that wound had faded to a wan dot, so that I'd have to search a bit to find its residue. But now the memento was sitting right next to a fresh scar, which brought it back to life and into stark relief.

As the cancer treatments plodded on, I looked forward to the day when my body might gather itself up, sprout hair on my head, and, I hoped, grow healthy cells. But for now, the disease forced me not only to face the painful realities of my family but also to look at myself—my actual body—and examine the collateral damage every single day. And the truly difficult part was the uncomfortable nexus of my cancer experience: how I saw myself as a woman, the need to finally acknowledge the iceberg I had been living inside of for most of my life, and the awareness of *who* had embedded me there.

A long if quiet trauma with my father had prevented any easiness in my body. I never saw it—nakedness—as a natural state. It was a condition, like an illness—a mistake, really, that had to be healed or rectified as quickly as possible. I was painfully shy as a child, and even before I'd gained, through the loose folds of my father's trousers, an encyclopedic knowledge of what an erect penis felt like (in all its various iterations, from slightly chubby to broom-handle hard and every degree in between), that bashfulness would continue to hound me as I became a young woman and throughout my adult life. I preferred loose-fitting clothing that hid my curves. Even in bed with men, I'd throw the covers back on top of us as fast as I thought was acceptable. Sex was indeed like doing hard time, counting the minutes, waiting to be released so I could turn away and relax back into the chill of the ice floe that encased my mind. Numbing myself in so many myriad and covert ways kept me at a distance from feeling *anything,* even when I was naked and at my most vulnerable. I'd been blind to my body since the day I told my father that I "understood" him. And with that nod of the head and just a few words, a girl's future potential, perhaps her most wanted desire—free and unfettered physical love—was sliced open, gutted out, and left for dead.

Now, with cancer, a *real* death threat, embedded into my breast, I was forced to literally look at them. *My breasts.* It was not an easy view.

So I didn't like this smaller, higher breast—or the other one, for that matter. And I didn't like the look of the flesh at my gut or the sick yellow chemo pallor under my eyes. My legs appeared to be shapeless stumps, my arms just conveniently placed appendages that could quickly cover up those ghastly bumps on my chest. I felt hideous.

I was uncharacteristically late that morning. Two children's concerts were scheduled for that afternoon, and I needed to get to the hall. I quickly dressed in concert black, but thinking of Donna and her red scarf the day before, I decided to wear red shoes for the trip to the hall and stuck a pair of black flats into my backpack for the performances.

Walking into the Sylvia and Danny Kaye Playhouse at Hunter College, I could hear the giggles and shouts of young children as their parents patiently tried to rein them in. I'd played this job, for the Little Orchestra Society, for years, and it was one of my favorites because the concerts exposed kids to classical music for perhaps the very first time.

The program that day was *Peter and the Wolf* by Sergey

Prokofiev, which I had performed dozens of times over many seasons. Throughout the concert, kids squealed nonstop. Looking into the audience and seeing the faces of children who might never before in their lives have heard a flute, a clarinet, a trumpet, or an oboe, much less an orchestra, was a privilege I never took for granted. I wasn't sure why, but the idea of giving this gift to them was especially poignant that day. Maybe it was because they were seeing me, and my eyes were open to them. I was looking, connecting, and understanding. And if I could begin to understand, then somehow I might also begin to forget. I felt a befuddling sense of happiness and somber resignation simultaneously.

The last notes sounded; the kids roared with applause. I'd play this exact show again in about an hour, and I wanted to get to the corner deli for a quick sandwich. But as I started to pack up my instrument, a mother and her small daughter made their way toward me. The stagehands rushed over to shoo them away, as union rules prohibited audience members from coming onto the stage. Putting my oboe on the chair beside me, I quickly walked over to the edge of the stage and knelt down to greet them.

"Did you like the concert today?"

The mom encouraged her shy daughter to answer my question.

"Yes."

"Emily, ask the lady what you want to know."

"What's your question, Emily?"

"What's that thing you're playing?"

"My instrument is called an oboe. I played the Duck in the performance. Did you hear that?"

"Yes."

"Emily, ask the lady..."

"Could *I* play the oboe?"

"Of course you could. But tell me, Emily. Why do you want to play the oboe?"

The girl thought for several seconds, then stared at me intently.

"Because I felt something strange."

I looked into this girl's confused eyes as she tried to articulate something that could not be clearly said, maybe even known. Giving her the chance to say it in her own words, I began to ask more questions.

"Ah...what did that strange thing feel like?"

"It was good..."

"Okay..."

I winked at the mother, who was looking at her daughter as if she were an alien from Mars. The little girl continued to struggle. "And it was...um, just good...I guess..."

"Good is great. But what *kind* of good? Can you tell me more about the *good?*"

"It was kind of *squishy*..."

Perfect. I took this shy girl's averted face between my hands and pulled her in toward me. Looking directly into her eyes, I passed along what Kirsten had given me when I was four years old.

"Well, Emily, that sounds like a perfect reason to play the oboe, because I'll tell you a little secret. That's exactly the same reason I became interested in music, too. Something felt *squishy.*"

Tristan und Isolde

As a freelancer, you find few opportunities to play opera. It's very expensive to mount productions outside the majestic venues: the New York City Opera (now, sadly, defunct) and the Metropolitan Opera. But one day a miracle happens. You get a call to play six three-hour rehearsals for a reading of Wagner's Tristan und Isolde. *Your very own Tristan! Your beloved Isolde!*

A few managers of "up-and-coming" and "rising star" opera singers are putting together the reading to generate exposure—and contracts—for their clients. You're hired to play English horn. This is so very exciting: you can now play Isolde's music. Kirsten's music. Your English horn solo will be the "shepherd's tune" in the third act, a sad and foreboding premonition of Tristan's death. At this moment in the opera the orchestra stops, and the English horn plays this solo for three long minutes.

Traditionally, many opera productions will require the player to come out of the pit, get into costume, and play the solo from memory onstage, as an actor. It is very dramatic. Tristan hears the shepherd's song and remembers how Isolde helped nurse him in battle. He looks to the sea for the ship that may carry her. With his eyes fixed on the horizon, he waits for her as he listens to the shepherd's plaintive tune. But in this rehearsal context, you will simply stand within the orchestra and play.

You prepare for two solid weeks, and it is a glorious event to anticipate. Everyone in the orchestra has given up better-paid work to accept this job. So the rehearsals begin—and the singers are great, and even the Italian conductor isn't bad. You go home every night and feel lucky that you have another day with Isolde to look forward to.

On the fifth day, however, they haven't even finished with the second act, and you begin to worry that you might not get to play the shepherd's tune after all. You worry that they might skip it altogether to save the three minutes of time. After all, it's not about you and your silly English horn solo! It's all about the singers. And in defense of them, why should they waste time on you and your shepherd's tune?

As you enter the rehearsal hall on the final day, you go into a deep protective space, girding yourself for the eventuality that they will skip your solo. After some playing and some waiting, they finally dive into the third act. The rehearsal has been extended an extra hour because the conductor realizes how badly he has planned. It's going along, and you are nervous: you just don't know what will happen.

Then they get to your spot in the music, the place of the shepherd's tune. Everyone stops and looks your way. The conductor nods. You get to your feet, pull the music stand up, take the correct breath, and begin. Your nerves calm down. Your hands stop shaking. The saliva comes back into your mouth. You take your time. You think fleetingly about Kirsten throughout the three minutes. You finish the solo. There is silence. The conductor says "Bis," which in Italian means "encore." He wants you to take three more valuable minutes and play it again! Everyone is looking at you, staring you down. You take your time, begin again. Again. For your Kirsten.

Red

LATE THAT AFTERNOON at the Kaye playhouse, after I'd played the second show, I thought of Emily. I worried that her mother would not understand just how profoundly music had touched her daughter. The sensation Emily felt, and was brave enough to verbalize, emerged from a miraculous, sweet place that would need attention from a loving parent, a parent who perhaps didn't understand but who was willing to learn along with her daughter. This opportunity could easily be missed by a mother who was too busy, a father who didn't care, or through simple neglect. Or worse.

Then I thought of all the freakish accidents and interactions that had somehow guided my own life. The brilliance of my mother's Hoover, which never seemed to drown out Kirsten's voice; switching from flute to oboe by simply acknowledging, in the moment, a powerful energy that compelled me to rise to my feet and volunteer—that is something I will always shake my head at in disbelief. There was a lot that went wrong, but I *was* saved; perhaps I'd saved myself. So I resolved to not worry about Emily. She'd probably be fine.

Lost in thought and butting up against some hard memories, I left the theater and walked without purpose, staring down at my red shoes. A Saturday on the Upper East Side at dinnertime left the streets fairly empty. I wandered, looking into the pricey shop windows, trying to guess the cost of various items that might be nice to own in another lifetime. But I moved forward, uptown and then eastward, trying to forget that little girl.

I found myself on East 74th Street just opposite the space where Mannes used to reside. The street still had that tony doyenne charm, but the music was long gone. In the mid-1980s Mannes had moved to the Upper West Side, into a larger facility. The row of connected town houses had been razed—a low, boxy residential building now stood in front of me. Staring at what should have been the school, I realized that Mrs. S.'s apartment building was behind me. It stood there, untouched. How many times had I raced across this very street to get to my classes straight from a fight with Whitney or from eavesdropping on Mrs. S. as she gossiped with Bitsy about Blabsy?

Feeling surrounded by my own distant but tender history, I felt a pulsing ache, like a bruise that had gone through its red-blue-purple stage and was about to turn that final ocher and heal. Sweat broke to the surface of my skin, and I adjusted the small backpack holding my oboe. It felt heavier across my shoulders and back than it should have. My stomach buckled, as though I had swallowed sour curdled milk. And then I remembered I'd had my chemo just the day before. Breathing deeply, I realized I couldn't remember whether I had walked down this street since I'd left Mannes in the late 1970s. Perhaps I *had* inadvertently, but I couldn't actually remember it, as if I were a determined amnesiac who wanted to forget the people I ran toward and from. As I stood there, the view was benign but also tinged with sweetness.

Kind of like when you return to a place you lived long ago, and the memory is huge, but when you go back, the room and the view are dwarfed, improbable.

I took the backpack off, set it on the ground, sat down in the middle of the lowest step to Mrs. S.'s building, and lay my head down onto my knees. I smelled the lotion and rubbed my forehead back and forth, deep into the skin. Then it came up—a dream from the night before. About my mother.

Honey, you can always move.

All of a sudden it was as if I were standing on 23rd Street and Seventh Avenue in the Chelsea of the 1970s. The southeast corner—darkly familiar. A screaming angel of a woman had interrupted my stutter step years ago on this very corner. In my dream, I turned around and around, gathering together each specter of my past. I looked west toward the Hudson River and could see everything with brilliant twenty-twenty vision all the way to New Jersey. And my hearing was also acute; I heard every breath each bird took and every secret, wisplike breeze the earth pushed my way. The weather was warm, balmy, and a breeze blew up against my lower back. My mother stepped out of the bodega on the opposite corner. As she strode confidently across the street in my direction, the cars swerved around her without slowing down. It all appeared to be a choreographed dance. She wore the shirtwaist dress of my childhood, her knees peeking out from below the hem. This was my mother of the pre-Hoover years—my mother before I met my Kirsten. This was the mother it was safe to love and who, I imagined, loved me in return—my mother from the page of a yearbook, smiling, with a crooked tooth. With her head canted in my general direction, she tossed the words to me as she strode by.

Honey, you can always move.

Honey. The throwaway endearment I had heard all my life.

You. Me, Marcia, her daughter.

Can. It is possible.

Always. Without exception.

Move.

"Miss? Excuse me. I need to get in here."

Someone was speaking, but my head felt cemented to my knees. When I opened my eyes, my red shoes came into focus, then the ground under them. I saw a pair of jeans and Nike sneakers with a red whoosh.

"Oh, sorry. I wasn't feeling well."

As I lifted my head up, the man, startled, quickly jumped back, as he clearly saw my unhealthy bald skull and sallow eyes. Inured to his reaction, I smiled and scooted to the side of the stoop.

"Can I get you something? I live on the first floor. Water?"

"No. I'm fine. Thanks. I was just resting for a minute."

"Well, take your time."

I was not a homeless lunatic, just a cancer patient. Relieved, he stepped by me and entered the building.

My hand was crimped shut and held stiff across my chest in a kind of deformed salute. Slowly I opened my fist and shook it out. I'd been there for some time, and I imagined—a bit sheepishly—all the other people who must have walked by and seen a bald woman curled into a ball on a stoop. Time to move. I grabbed my oboe bag, slung it on my back, and walked east. As I was crossing Third Avenue, something caught my eye. Something red. I walked in that direction, feeling pushed, pulled, beckoned.

Dusk was falling, and my long shadow stretched out in front of me. My skull looked like a dot on a clothespin; the sun pressed heavily at my neck. Turning to look behind me, I saw the beginnings of a red sunset, which boded well for sailors—their morning delight. The next day would be clear, sunny—perhaps hopeful. And now this wondrous thing directly above me flapped vigorously in the strong, gusting wind. I stopped dead in my tracks and looked up. A red cloth banner extended from a pole attached to a building with huge glass doors.

Just then, I understood that red *was* the most luscious color in the world. A resonating, resounding, and restorative color that infuses and organizes the universe, like the sound waves of music that rule our local and distant solar systems. With the fabric swirling above me, in front of me, all around me, I heard the red's melody, and I felt its rhythm pound against my chest.

My sweat, still sticky, had almost dried up, and I could now smell myself. Exhausted and possibly insane, I looked into this building, pressed my nose to the glass door, and saw people milling about, strolling from wall to wall. White papers were plastered onto those walls, and the color red was prominent, popping out—perhaps art, though I couldn't be sure. Someone in a tuxedo, a waiter, it seemed, was filling tulip glasses with bubbly, and occasionally someone raised a glass in a toast. I imagined they were celebrating the red. Words were said; I couldn't hear; didn't care.

For more time than was surely appropriate, I stood looking into what must have been a private event. I was not invited, yet I felt tethered to these people, who, I imagined, also loved the red. Everything whirled and shimmered—the flapping red banner above me, the red sky behind me, my red shoes below me, and the red splashes I felt inside. All around, red flowed freely and surrounded my vacant heart. With both hands placed firmly on the crystal-clear glass door, I pushed forward, opened my heart, and walked into the red.

Amnesia — A Love Story

For many years you work hard to forget. Complete amnesia the goal. It's not easy or always successful, but after a time the memories you seek to avoid recede, and in their place you gain some manner of neutrality. You're not cold, exactly, but you've managed a reprieve from the sad heat that used to burn your heart. To the touch, you are cool.

One day while you're taking a break, watching a midday soap opera, you hear the postman drop a particularly heavy parcel through the slot of your front door. It lands with a beckoning thump. Curious, you step into the mudroom and see the handwriting—distinctive fat loops, unchanged over time. You rip it open. It's a book—a memoir. She's written about her life, and after ten years of silence it seems your mother wants to tell you something.

But you don't want to read. You don't want to bring back the hope that nailed you to your cross of wanting, which you carried on your back from the age of zero. The book, a self-published affair, feels radioactive, as though its very presence will poison you and give you cancer again. So you pick it up by the corner and quickly, before it explodes, run into the kitchen and throw it into the garbage bin. Over the next few days it remains buried under an ever-increasing pile of coffee grounds, eggshells, uneaten toast, and other rotting items. It's just plain old nonrecyclable refuse.

You hold off taking out the garbage. That toxic ream of paper seems to glow every time you enter the kitchen. And finally, because the garbage is beginning to reek, you reach down through the clotted food to retrieve the book. You wipe off the bits of grounds and yolk and stains as best you can. Now, you tell yourself, you're ready to read what she wants you to know; certainly information known and unknown, maybe her secrets, but perhaps an answer that will allow you to become warm again; a woman who has a mother.

So you begin to read, slowly, deliberately. But mostly you're looking. You're searching for your name. And as you read her words you begin to skim and turn the pages faster, your eyes becoming robot eyes, scanning the white paper and the black ink looking for the letter M. Until you get to the end, when you understand that your name is not there. She's written a memoir and has not mentioned her children. And then she sent it to you. That's what she wanted you to know: while you were forgetting her, she'd also forgotten you. So you go back to the tight cool corner that keeps you sane. You make believe she's dead so that there's no possibility that anything she does or writes or doesn't do or doesn't write can ever break your heart again.

Your father dies. You're aware of feeling nothing. And then you get a call a few years later that she's died, too. You feel an enormous, bloated nothing. Silence over many years has helped, but with this added layer of death, you feel free from them both. But mostly from her.

Then your brain begins to ooze from its weep holes. You re-member what you forgot to forget. The odor of Mrs. Paul's fried scallops late at night. Creeping down the hall to find her in the kitchen with the lights blazing, reading a mystery with a scary skull and crossbones on the spine. Crawling into her lap in the middle of those late nights and sticking your nose into her face to get an unforgettable whiff of seafood and Pall Malls and Jergens lotion. Your love of her smell. Perhaps she forgot to forget that also. And Mother, if you remembered this, too, did you also remember that you loved me?

Acknowledgments

Effusive thanks to my agents, Susan Feldstein and Paul Feldstein, who responded in less than five minutes to an out-of-the-blue query (is there any other kind?) from a former oboe-playing, not-so-sure writer, asking for my complete manuscript. We signed two months later.

I will be forever grateful for the honor of working with my brilliant Little, Brown editor, Vanessa Mobley, who not only managed to convince me that I am, in fact, a writer but also demonstrated that she knows my voice better than I do. I cannot imagine a kinder, more attuned editor than Vanessa.

At Little, Brown, my publisher, Reagan Arthur, and my production editor, Pamela Marshall.

My copyeditor, Barbara Clark.

Thanks for kind and generous assistance: Catherine Michelle Adams, Adrienne Brodeur, Ann Chou, Terril Gagnier, Constantine Kitsopoulos, Ralph Olsen, Charles Salzberg, Peter Weitzner, and the New York Writers Workshop. And particularly my dear friend Tim Page, whom I've known since our days at Mannes. He read and encouraged and supported me throughout the writing of this book.

I am so grateful to Dr. Howard Welsh, who helped me to locate my bravery.

And finally, endless thanks for the greatest gifts given to me:

Kirsten Flagstad, whose voice resounds forever in the air.

Mrs. S., wherever you are.

The former titans of the old 74th Street Mannes College of Music.

The red-haired woman on 23rd Street who pushed me.

The 1 a.m. strollers in Central Park who ignored me.

The doctors who saved me.

Thank you all. Madly, truly, deeply.

About the Author

Marcia Butler was a professional oboist for twenty-five years until her retirement from music in 2008. During her musical career, she performed as a principal oboist and soloist on the most renowned New York and international stages and with many high-profile musicians and orchestras—including pianist André Watts, composer and pianist Keith Jarrett, and soprano Dawn Upshaw. She lives in New York City.